Battleground Europe
Airfields and Airmen
Arras

These, in the day when heaven was falling,
The hour when earth's foundations fled,
Followed their mercenary calling
And took their wages and are dead.

Their shoulders held the sky suspended;
They stood, and earth's foundations stay;
What God abandoned, these defended,
And saved the sum of things for pay.

A E Housman

Battleground Europe

Airfields and Airmen
Arras

Mike O'Connor

Series editor
Nigel Cave

Pen & Sword
MILITARY

To Claire (Weed) and Ian (Een Boy), my children (a.k.a. the Ankle
Biters, Heirs to the Overdraft, Little Blighters, etc) who I love dearly.

First published in 2004, by
PEN & SWORD MILITARY
an imprint of
Pen & Sword Books Limited
47 Church Street, Barnsley, South Yorkshire S70 2AS

ISBN 1 84415 125 5

A CIP catalogue record for this book
is available from the British Library.

Printed and bound in Great Britain by
CPI UK

Pen & Sword Books Ltd incorporates the imprints of
Pen & Sword Aviation, Pen & Sword Maritime, Pen & Sword Military,
Wharncliffe Local History, Pen & Sword Select,
Pen & Sword Military Classics and Leo Cooper.

For a complete list of Pen & Sword titles please contact:
PEN & SWORD BOOKS LIMITED
47 Church Street, Barnsley, South Yorkshire, S70 2AS, England.
E-mail: enquiries@pen-and-sword.co.uk
Website: www.pen-and-sword.co.uk

Cover Painting: By Colin Ashford GAvA. The picture depicts Flight Lieutenant C D
Booker of 8 Naval Squadron, based at Mont-St-Éloi, in his Sopwith Triplane N5482
'Maud', shooting down *Oberleutnant* Adolf Ritter von Tutschek, commander of Jasta
12. Tutschek, who had been awarded the *Pour le Mérite,* was severely wounded. He
was killed in action on 15 March 1918. See page 125 and *Airfields and Airmen:
Somme* page 66.

CONTENTS

INTRODUCTION BY SERIES EDITOR

Airfields and Airmen: Arras is the fourth in this excellent addition to the Battleground Europe series. It cannot be an easy task to have envisaged how to bring the stories of men whose actions were into the air down to the ground in the form of a battlefield guide. But the last few books, on Ypres, the Somme and Cambrai, have shown that it is indeed a practicable proposition.

As I said in an introduction to an earlier book, I have never been greatly interested in the war in the air - nothing to do with the subject, just a quirk of preference! But one undeniably striking fact is that the development of aircraft in the few years after that ever so short initial flight in late 1903 went ahead at an extraordinary rate. It is regrettable, as with so many areas of technology, that effective weapons of war and the military needs of the combatant nations ensured such a rapid technological development, because funding and resources became almost unlimited.

It is fortunate that there has been so much work by devoted historians to uncover as much information as they can of the war in the air - and to make it available in excellent books - so that we know so much about the conflict in the skies. Log books, the relatively small size of squadrons and, perhaps, the nature of the men involved, have ensured a wealth not only of combat detail but of insights into individuals. When this is combined with the individual nature of the combats, with a couple of men in a machine and relatively few aircraft involved in even the most complex of fights, the result is that many airmen have given us a legacy of the air war that is in many ways much more detailed than the fighting experience of their comrades engaged on the ground and at sea. The fortitude shown by fighting people elsewhere was no less, but the nature of aerial combat and the organisation surrounding the air arm, ensures that, generally, we have a clearer vision of the fighting man.

These airmen, of all nationalities, serve as a type for all those who fought and suffered in the Great War - and, by extension, to conflicts beyond. Placing them on the ground - the location of their airfields, their careers in France and Flanders and, all too often their resting place, brings a new dimension which can only enhance our understanding and our respect.

Nigel Cave
Archivi Centrale dell'Istituto della Carità
Stresa

ACKNOWLEDGEMENTS

This volume of *Airfields and Airmen* books is again only possible due to the help of my many friends.

Once more I am eternally grateful for the enormous help and encyclopaedic knowledge of Alex Imrie and for all his German photographs in the book.

I would also like to thank Jon Wilkinson of Pen and Sword, who has done yet another splendid job on the book layout.

My next thanks have to go to the unpaid members of *Jasta* 99, Jim Davies, Barry Gray and Richard Owen. Jim has toiled away navigating and writing directions for this book and Barry has produced nearly all of the images, spending thankless hours in his darkroom. Richard eventually solved the mystery of H H Bright.

I would also like to thank the following: Colin Ashford GAvA for his usual splendid cover illustration; Paul Baillie; Simon Baugh; Baron and Baronne Becquet de Megille; Nigel Cave; Dan Cippico, nephew of Francis Mond; Ann Clayton; the staff of the Commonwealth War Graves Commission at Beaurains; Sue Cox; Gerry and Ann Crole; M and Mme Louis Flinois-Bassery; Norman Franks; the German War Graves Commission; Hal Giblin; Barry Greenwood; Christine Gregory, latterly of the RAF Museum; Tim Harper; Trevor Henshaw; Phil Jarrett; Jeff Jefford; Peter Kilduff; Stuart Leslie for his enormous help with photographs; Raymond Loyer-Leroy; Bob Lynes; Joe Michie; Raymond Mignot; Julian Mitchell for his assistance with his great-uncle S J Mitchell; Simon Moody, also latterly of the RAF Museum; the Earl of Moray; Captain Carlos Nunes, Defence Attaché at the Portuguese Embassy and the staff of the *Arquivo da Força Aérea;* the staff at Pen and Sword; the staff of the Public Record Office; Keith Rennles; Alex Revell; the staff of the *Service Historique de l'Armée del'Air*; William Spencer; Brian Sperring; Stewart K Taylor; Alan Wakefield of the Imperial War Museum; Colin Waugh; Brigadier Henry Wilson; Lawrie Woodcock and Neville Wridgway

Every effort has been made to contact the authors of the various books or articles quoted and their copyright is acknowledged.

INTRODUCTION

This volume, the fourth in the *Airfields and Airmen* series, covers the area to the north of the Somme and Cambrai books and encompasses a larger area. The tours feature the first operational loss by the RFC, the graves of Albert Ball VC and James McCudden VC. There are also visits to a number of interesting German sites and cemeteries.

Cross referencing notes in the text

As the *Airfields and Airmen* series has expanded more points of interest have become interlinked. It has been necessary to include more notes in the text referring the reader to incidents or places in the other books. This also refers readers to volumes not yet published. In order for this not to be intrusive or interrupt the flow of the narrative I have abbreviated where possible. Thus instead of writing, for example, See *Airfields and Airmen: Ypres* page 147, this has now been reduced to *Ypres*, page 147.

The military background of the Arras area

The town of Arras occupies a very strategic place, being situated in a gap through the hills and is the hub of roads, railways and waterways. In October 1914 the situation in the area settled down to trench warfare with the French occupying the strategically important objective of Arras and the Germans in possession of the high ground to the north. In March 1915 the French attempted to take the high ground with an attack on the Lorette spur at the northern end of the ridge by the village of Souchez. By the late autumn they were in possession of Lorette and had forced their way up the long slope of Vimy Ridge but were still 200 feet below the crest. Their casualties were enormous with 150,000 men killed, missing or wounded. The National Cemetery at Notre-Dame de Lorette, dominates the area and stands as a reminder of this great sacrifice. In March 1916 the British army took over this part of the front and found the area full of the remains of French soldiers.

The most important event for the British on this part of the front was the Battle of Arras which commenced on 9 April 1917 and was in support of the French offensive further south on the Aisne. The highlight of the battle was the capture of Vimy Ridge by the Canadian Corps, which historically in some ways has largely overshadowed the main operation. The RFC's part was important and they had learned vital lessons from the Battle of the Somme the previous summer, particularly in wireless, artillery co-operation and tactics. Unfortunately, they had fallen behind the Germans in quality of aeroplanes and were awaiting better equipment in the shape of the Sopwith Camel, SE5 and Bristol Fighter. The Germans on the other hand were re-equipping with the formidable Albatros scout. In maintaining the offensive policy British casualties were dreadful and the month became known to the RFC as Bloody April.

In March 1917 the Germans withdrew to a new prepared position, known to the British as the Hindenburg Line, in order to shorten their line and conserve resources. This had the effect of upsetting the French plans. In the event, the Nivelle Second Aisne offensive failed and the loss of morale in the French army resulted in mutinies.

Compared to the Somme movement of the front line in this area was quite small and Vimy Ridge, together with Arras, remained a bastion of the British line and was to withstand the German onslaught of March 1918.

THE GUIDE

There have been many guides to the various battlefields of the Western Front, some of them extremely detailed, but there have not been any concerning the flying aspect. Using old photographs, maps and contemporary accounts I visited old aerodrome sites and was amazed how little many of them had changed. You can hold up an old photograph of some of them and the scene behind today appears only to lack the aeroplanes. In fact many of the farms associated with these aerodromes have probably changed little in two or three hundred years.

For the military historian most of the First War has a convenient chronological and geographical sequence in that one can relate how far a battle progressed (or not as the case may be) on a day-by-day basis. The air war unfortunately does not fit into this tidy pattern. Squadrons or flights would take off from one point, have a fight or range an artillery battery at another and casualties would be spread all over the front, on both sides and many miles behind the actual fighting. Casualties from a single air battle might be buried in different cemeteries miles apart.

This guide has attempted to link interesting events and individuals together, into some sort of logical and digestible order, despite the differences in time and geography. The choice of personalities and

9

events is purely my idea of what is interesting. There has always been the glamour of the scout or fighter pilot and the 'aces' and in recent years there has been what I consider an unhealthy obsession with trying to discover 'who shot down whom'. This at best is a risky past-time, taking into account the confused nature of an air battle, the fallibility of human memory and the marked absence of German records. The air war was not just about aces but involved all the mundane tasks of photography, reconnaissance, artillery ranging, bombing, tank co-operation, infantry co-operation, supply dropping and all the myriad tasks that enabled the Allied armies to win the war. To concentrate on just one aspect of the aerial battle does not do justice to the rest.

However in a book of this kind one cannot ignore the 'aces' theme, though I use the information of 'who got who' advisedly and would hope that I have presented a reasonably balanced picture of what the first air war was like.

The Commonwealth War Graves Commission

The Commission never fails to impress me and any praise for them is too little. They care for my grandfather (and my mother) and maintain the beautiful cemeteries with what seems a ridiculously small workforce. I have trouble keeping my garden under control and yet they maintain acres of manicured grass and lovely flower beds to perfection, with a mere handful of staff.

I would urge all visitors to the cemeteries to record their comments in the Visitors Book, for this not only shows the Commission and its staff that their work is appreciated but it also keeps alive the memory of the thousands of servicemen buried there.

HOW THE GUIDE WORKS

At the beginning of the guide is a map of the entire area covered by this volume. On it are marked the major towns and the aerodromes, with an overlap so that the reader can also relate places to features that appear in other volumes.

THE TOURS AND DIRECTIONS

For all aerodrome entries there is an associated plan, with present day buildings annotated. This should enable the reader to orientate himself. Also noted, are the locations of some of the buildings and other features that once stood there. On the plans there are arrows that are aligned with present day photographs, which explain more fully the layout and views you can expect to see. The arrow has a number alongside it referring to the relevant photograph. Some of the aerodromes have disappeared under housing estates and industrial complexes and require a little imagination on the part of the visitor. Many of the points of interest that you can visit were established on farms or near chateaux. They are of interest to you and me but please remember that these are private residences and they do not like hordes of visitors crossing their property any more than you would. Please respect their privacy and use your discretion.

AERODROMES

For all aerodrome entries there is an associated plan, with present day buildings annotated. This should enable the reader to orientate himself. Also noted, are the locations of some of the buildings and other features that once stood there. On every plan there are arrows that are aligned with present day photographs, which explain more fully the layout and views you can expect to see. The arrow has a number alongside it referring to the relevant photograph. Certain aerodromes will require considerable imagination, such as Hesdigneul, where so much has disappeared under housing estates and industrial complexes.

Many of the points of interest that you can visit were established on farms or near châteaux. They are of interest to you and me but please remember that these are private residences and they do not like hordes of visitors crossing their property any more than you would. Please respect their privacy and use your discretion.

CEMETERIES

In each cemetery entry I have given the Commonwealth War Graves reference number, as it appears on the yellow 1/200,000 Michelin map, so that if you become lost as a result of my directions, you can at least navigate to the relevant location. The reference is given as the map section, followed by the cemetery number (i.e. 2/28 is Cabaret Rouge British Cemetery which is cemetery No. 28 in section 2.)

At the time of writing (January 2004) these overprinted maps have been discontinued and will only last as long as stocks remain. However, the good news is that the Commonwealth War Graves Commission are about to publish a book of maps indicating cemetery locations. Each cemetery will have its own number, unlike the yellow maps where numbers could be different where there was an overlap between adjoining sheets.

At each cemetery the pertinent grave numbers are given, so that the visitor has a starting point for not only the individual involved but the section of associated text. I would suggest that you view the cemetery register and locate the grave to be visited, as the orientation of some cemeteries can be confusing to start with.

TABLE OF MAPS

THE DEVELOPMENT OF MILITARY FLYING

Great Britain

Early Days

Military experiments with balloons began at Woolwich Arsenal in 1878 and a balloon section participated in the Aldershot manoeuvres of 1880 and 1882. These were judged a success with the result that a Balloon Equipment Store was set up at Woolwich by the Royal Engineers to manufacture balloons, instruct in ballooning and serve as a Depot.

In 1883 the Store was transferred to the Royal Engineers Depot at Chatham and was renamed the Balloon School and Factory.

During Sir Charles Warren's expedition to Bechuanaland in 1884 three balloons were employed with a force of two officers and fifteen NCOs and other ranks. After this episode, however, little official interest was displayed and it was only the efforts of a few enlightened officers which kept military ballooning alive. For example, experiments in observing gun fire were carried out, mainly with captive balloons. In 1890 a balloon section was introduced into the army as a part of the Royal Engineers and two years later the centre of balloon work was moved to Aldershot. During the Boer War in 1899 four sections were employed and carried out useful work in directing artillery fire and observation, despite unfavourable conditions and not a little prejudice. In 1905 a better site at South Farnborough was chosen and this evolved into what became the Royal Aircraft Factory (later re-titled the Royal Aircraft Establishment to avoid confusion with the Royal Air Force) and the site of the famous Farnborough air shows. In 1911 the Air Battalion of the Royal Engineers was formed and the Balloon School at Farnborough became No.1 Company and No.2 Company, with aeroplanes, moved to Larkhill in Wiltshire.

The Royal Aircraft Factory

The aeroplane experiments of two aviation pioneers, Lieutenant William Dunne and Mr Samuel Cody, were encouraged by Colonel Capper, superintendent of the balloon factory, despite very meagre financial resources. In September of 1907 the first British army airship, Nulli Secundus, flew at the Factory. Cody was involved with this and had been supplying man carrying kites to the Factory since 1904. The Factory carried out research into all aspects of aeronautics and did much to standardise component parts of aeroplanes. The value of this was demonstrated during the war when a host of furniture and wagon making companies could be subcontracted to manufacture aeroplanes or aeroplane parts. There was criticism from some areas that the Factory was a government monopoly and this came to a head in 1916 with the so-called 'Fokker Scourge' when British losses increased considerably due to obsolete machines. These had been largely products of the Factory. Friction arose as the Factory felt it should supervise and co-ordinate the efforts of the private makers, whilst the independent aeroplane makers feared the paralysing effect of officialdom.

Private enterprise

The British had taken up aviation rather late and were well behind France and Germany. The Royal Aero Club had been formed in 1901 and issued its first Aero Certificate to a qualified pilot, J T C Moore-Brabazon, in March 1910. The first, recognised, powered flight in Britain had been made by Cody in 1908 using a self-built machine, and in 1911 Tom Sopwith had also built his own aircraft, having previously flown mainly French and American designs. He acquired premises at Kingston where during the First World War thousands of his aircraft were built, including the legendary Sopwith Camel. There was no shortage of enthusiasm, though most of the early pioneers were reasonably well to do, and were spending their own money. By the beginning of the First World War there was a host of aircraft manufacturers, some of them quite small and many destined not to survive the post -war collapse of the aviation industry. Geoffrey De Havilland built his first machine in 1910 but later that year joined the government Royal Aircraft Factory. The main centre for civil aviation was the motor racing circuit at Brooklands where A V Roe had made his inaugaral flight, though there were other centres like Eastchurch, and Claude Graham White's works at Hendon (now the home of the Royal Air Force Museum).

The Creation of the Royal Flying Corps

The lack of official interest and progress in aviation, was continually highlighted by the aviation press, and eventually the government was forced to act. A sub-committee of the Imperial Committee of Defence recommended the creation of a British Aeronautical Service and this came into existence on 13 April 1912. It was called the Royal Flying Corps and was to consist of a Military Wing, a Naval Wing and a Central Flying School. The old No.1 Company became No.1 Squadron and No.2 Company became No. 2 Squadron. In theory it was a combined military and naval air service, but in practice it was doomed to failure with split control. The Naval Wing continued to do its own thing, ultimately becoming the separate Royal Naval Air Service (RNAS).

Between 1912 and the outbreak of war the RFC carried out considerable experimental work in co-operation with the army, aerial photography, bombing, wireless telegraphy and photography.

In the army manoeuvres of 1912 each of the two opposing forces were supplied with an RFC squadron. The defending side was able to use air reconnaissance to locate the attacking force, commanded by General Douglas Haig, whilst the cavalry had been unable to do so - and in a fraction of the time. Grierson, commanding the defending force, used aeroplanes for reconnaissance for the rest of the manoeuvres.

The Royal Naval Air Service

The Royal Navy initially showed interest in airships for the protection of trade routes due to the apparent lack of performance and promise of aeroplanes. After a disastrous start, when their first airship broke its back before even flying, interest quietly lapsed. However, in 1911 a patriotic pioneer pilot, Francis McClean, who owned the site of the flying field at Eastchurch on the Isle of Sheppey, offered to loan two of his machines to train four RN officers. George Cockburn, another pioneer pilot, offered to train them free of charge and Short's provided free technical assistance at their factory. Short Brothers had their factory at Battersea but later opened another at Eastchurch and became almost the exclusive supplier of seaplanes to the RNAS. Later in 1911 McClean bought another ten acres at Eastchurch and gave it to the Royal Navy to set up their own flying school. Much experimentation was carried out with wireless, seaplanes and flying aeroplanes from ships. Shortly before the war the Navy revived its interest in airships ordering several from different manufacturers, including some from Germany, and in January 1914 airships became the exclusive preserve of the Royal Navy. By the beginning of the war the RNAS had established a number of bases round the coast of Britain.

To War

In June 1914 the RFC concentrated all its squadrons at Netheravon. The mornings were given over to trials and experiments and the afternoons to lectures and discussions. Reconnaissance, photography and moving landing grounds were all practiced, and plans for mobilization were also formulated. Four days were allowed for this, with a move to France on the sixth day.

War came in August 1914. At its declaration No.2 Squadron made the epic flight down from their base at Montrose in Scotland, and yet 2, 3 and 4 Squadrons were all at Dover by the evening of 12 August, with 5 Squadron arriving two days later. 6 Squadron was given the job of preparing the aerodrome at Dover and some of their personnel made up the numbers of the other squadrons. The squadrons crossed the Channel on the morning of 13 August. There had been meticulous planning for this operation with all the support transport collected at Regents Park and consisting of motor cars and commercial vehicles still in the gaudy colour schemes of their previous owners.

The RFC was a tiny force of 276 officers and 1797 other ranks - about half the size of an infantry brigade. It took to the field with virtually all of its available resources and the aeroplanes left behind were largely worn out or scrap. In command of the RFC was Brigadier General David Henderson, who had fought at Khartoum in 1898 and distinguished himself during the Boer War. He had learned to fly at Brooklands at the grand age of 49 and over the next four years was probably the most influential force on the development of British air power.

The four squadrons collected at Maubeuge on 16 August and for two or three days relatively little happened. On Wednesday 18 August the first historic reconnaissance was flown by P B Joubert de La Ferte, in a Bleriot of 3 Squadron and G W Mapplebeck in a BE2 of 4 Squadron. Both became completely lost in cloud but were able to return later unscathed. The RFC quickly proved its worth and on 22 August large bodies of enemy troops were spotted advancing on the British line. During the retreat from Mons the squadrons moved from field to field, moving in all about ten times in as many days. In particular the RFC spotted von Kluck's attempt to outflank the British Expeditionary Force and the signal was taken personally by Henderson to British Headquarters.

After the Battle of the Marne and the so-called 'Race to the Sea' the RFC moved north with the rest of the British Army and set up headquarters at St Omer, where they soon settled into the pattern that would remain for the rest of the war. With the advent of static trench warfare the style of operation involved mapping enemy trench systems and fortifications, ranging artillery using wireless, photography and bombing. In November 1914 F H Sykes, who was in charge of the RFC at the time, decentralized the RFC and grouped 2 and 3 Squadrons to make 1 Wing, with 5 and 6 Squadrons comprising 2 Wing, each responsible to First and Second Armies respectively.

Expansion

With the massive increase of the British forces on the Western Front there came the last significant change in the RFC structure when, on 30 January 1916, Wings were grouped to make Brigades. A Brigade would consist of a Corps Wing, whose squadrons were dedicated to particular artillery formations in their Army, and an Army Wing with fighter squadrons, whose job was to clear the air of enemy machines and protect the Corps aircraft. By the end of the war a Brigade could have more than two Wings, and as the British army took over more of the line from the French further Brigades were formed to support the newly created Armies. Each was a self-supporting organization with its own Aircraft Park for issuing new machines, its own Kite Balloon Wing and all the other ancillary units such as ammunition columns, lorry parks.

The Royal Air Force

The public outcry about the German air raids on Britain, particularly the daylight aeroplane raids of the summer of 1917, forced the government to completely re-appraise the whole question of the air services. A committee under the great South African statesman Lieutenant General Jan Christian Smuts examined all aspects of air policy and organization. The main feature was to be the establishment of an independent air service by the amalgamation of the RFC and RNAS into a single force, the Royal Air Force, on 1 April 1918. One of the main driving forces during this process was Lieutenant General Sir David Henderson. There was much grumbling from the independent RNAS concerning the loss of their naval terminology and tradition, but nevertheless it worked and many ex-RNAS officers reached the highest ranks of the RAF.

Germany

Zeppelins and balloons

The German experience in many ways was similar to the British, though they utilized airships, particularly the rigid *Zeppelin* type, to a much greater degree.

In 1884 the Prussian Army set up a detachment to examine the use of balloons and by 1901 this had grown to two Companies. Like the RFC they used spherical balloons both tethered and free, but then moved onto the sausage-shaped kite balloon similar to the observation balloons used in the First War. Even though most of their efforts were directed at airships, in October 1908 the General Staff set up a technical section to observe various areas, including aviation. The War Ministry, bowing to the suggestions of the General Staff, authorised financial help to the most promising of the private aeroplane constructors. A prize of 40,000 marks was put up in 1908 for the first flight by a German aeroplane and this was won in October of that year at Johannisthal near Berlin.

Aeroplane development

The *Albatros Werke* put an aeroplane and a pilot at the disposal of the military, much the same way as Francis McClean had done with the Royal Navy at Eastchurch, and by March 1911 ten pilots had been trained. As a result of a military commission investigating various types of machines seven were eventually purchased. At the army manoeuvres of 1911 aeroplanes gained valuable experience but the army was still more concerned with balloons. Fortunately for the Germans the Chief of the General Staff, General von Moltke, was a far-sighted officer and in 1912 proposed detailed plans of how the aviation services should be organized.

The War Ministry was still concerned, however, that the promise of heavier than air flying could suffer a setback and that the flying services were receiving more attention than they should. However these plans did start to come together in October 1913 when *Oberst* von Eberhardt became the first *Inspekteur der Fliegertruppen* on the formation of the office of *Inspektion der Fliegertruppen* (abbreviated to *Idflieg*). Considerable training and expense went in to the *Fliegertruppe* from this date up to mobilization on 1 August 1914.

The German air organisation

At the outbreak of war there were thirty three *Feldflieger Abteilungen* (field flying companies) with six machines each, with another ten allocated to the fortress towns of Germany, plus twenty three balloon units and twelve army airships, most of which were unsuitable for operations. Each of the eight German Armies were allocated a balloon unit and one *Feldflieger Abteilung*, with another to each Corps. The airships were kept under the control of Army High Command, but due to a variety of factors their numbers were halved within a month and they were never actually used for reconnaissance in the West. The Army High Command was entitled the *Obersten Heeresleitung*, which was abbreviated *OHL*.

The German air service, like their RFC counterparts, operated a mixed collection of machines, and not until the middle of 1916 did the two-seater units have an aeroplane with a forward firing gun for the pilot and a ring mounted machine gun for the observer at the back. These were designated C-type machines. In addition the Germans were the first to utilise the fixed machine gun synchronised to fire through the propeller. An aircraft equipped with this feature, the single-seater Fokker monoplane, was able to maintain aerial supremacy from mid 1915 until the Spring of 1916.

By March 1915 the number of *Feldflieger Abteilung* had more than doubled and specialist units were being developed. The bomber force was eventually amalgamated into *Kampfgeschwader der Obersten Heeresleitung* or *Kagohl* (ie *Ka* of the *OHL*) and five of these units were formed.

The first fighter squadrons

Initially the Fokker monoplanes were allocated to two-seater units in twos or threes but for the Battle of Verdun in 1916 they were reorganized into three *Kommandos*. In August 1916 they became *Jagdstaffeln* (hunting squadrons, abbreviated to *Jastas*). Equipped with the new biplane D-type single-seat machines replacing the out-dated E-type monoplanes, and with a strength of a dozen aeroplanes, these *Jastas* were the first true German fighter units. Finally in October the position of *Kommandierenden General der Luftstreitkrafte (Kogenluft)* was created and was now responsible for all German flying units (except the German navy and

Bavarian ones) including training and reported directly to the Chief of the General Staff of Armies in the Field. This was the formation of the German Army Air Service.

All flying units were re-organised and the old *Feldflieger Abteilung* became *Flieger Abteilung* and the artillery units were re-designated *Flieger Abteilung* (A). The former carried out long range reconnaissance for army headquarters and the latter the duties of infantry co-operation and artillery observation. Units were no longer responsible to individual Corps but allocated to each Army and as such were very similar to the shape and operation of the British Brigade system that had evolved a few months earlier. The head of each Army's flying units was titled *Kommandeur der Flieger (Kofl)*.

The *Amerikaprogamm*

With the entry of the United States into the war Germany realized that American industry would soon be a deciding factor and a decision must be forced before this happened. The flying services embarked on a major expansion, which they called the *Amerikaprogramm*, calling for an increase of forty *Jagdstaffeln* and seventeen *Flieger Abteilung (A)*, in addition to massive increases in aircraft production and training. In June 1917 *Jastas* were grouped together into *Jagdgeschwader*, when *Jastas* 4, 6, 10 and 11 combined to form *Jagdgeschwader* 1. The target of forty fighter units was achieved but in practice most were only up to half strength and in the end the two-seater units increased by only six of the projected seventeen, though the strength of some others was increased.

In March 1918 the German army launched its last great offensive to try and obtain a breakthrough before the might of the American forces could become decisive. The use of new tactics and the new reserves, brought from the Eastern Front, very nearly triumphed. Losses in the *Luftstreitkräfte*, or German Air Service, were high.

The End

In June 1918 *Kogenluft* produced another expansion plan but German industry was unable to meet these targets, due to the lack of raw materials. The training of pilots and observers could also not keep up with demand. Finally, the Allied blockade reduced the amount of fuel that German aeroplanes were able to use. At the Armistice on 11 November 1918 the German army had some 280 flying units and a personnel total of about 4,500, which was considerably less than the RAF. Nevertheless, it had been effective in the way it had been employed.

Under the terms of the Armistice the German air service handed over all its fighters and bombers and though some aeroplanes were used in fighting on the Eastern front during 1919 it was officially disbanded in May 1920.

German ranks and their British equivalent

German army

German	British
Oberst	Colonel
Rittmeister	Cavalry Captain
Hauptmann	Army Captain
Oberleutnant	Lieutenant
Leutnant	Second Lieutenant
Fähnrich	Officer Cadet
Offizierstellvertreter	Warrant Officer
Feldwebel	Sergeant Major
Vizefeldwebel	No British equivalent
Unteroffizier	Corporal
Gefreiter	Private (First Class)
Flieger	Enlisted man
Pionier	Bavarian rank for Flieger

German navy

German	British
Kapitän	Captain
Kapitänleutnant	Lieutenant Commander
Oberleutnant zur See	Lieutenant
Leutnant zur See	Sub Lieutenant
Oberflugmeister	Chief Petty Officer
Flugmeister	Petty Officer

Abbreviations

AEO	Assistant Equipment Officer
AFC	Air Force Cross
AFC	Australian Flying Corps
BE	Bleriot Experimental
CB	Companion of the Bath
CBE	Commander of the Order of the British Empire
CMG	Companion of the Order of St Michael and St George
CO	Commanding Officer
CVO	Commander of the Royal Victorian Order
CWGC	Commonwealth War Graves Commission
DCM	Distinguished Conduct Medal
DFC	Distinguished Flying Cross
DFM	Distinguished Flying Medal
DH	De Havilland
DSC	Distinguished Service Cross
DSO	Distinguished Service Order
EA	Enemy aircraft
FA	*Flieger Abteilung*
FA(A)	*Flieger Abteilung(A)*
FE	Farman Experimental
FEA	*Flieger Ersatz Abteilung*
FB	Fighting Biplane
GC	Group Captain
GCB	Knight Grand Cross of the Bath
GCMG	Knight Grand Cross of the Order of St Michael and St George
HA	Hostile Aircraft
JG	*Jagdgeschwader*
KB	Kite Balloon
KBE	Knight Commander of the Order of the British Empire
KCB	Knight Commander of the Order of the Bath
KG	Knight of the Order of the Garter
LVG	*Luft-Verkehrs-Gesellschaft*
MC	Military Cross
NCO	Non Commissioned Officer
OC	Officer Commanding
OM	Order of Merit
POW	Prisoner of War
RAF	Royal Air Force
RAS	Reserve Aeroplane Squadron
RE	Reconnaissance Experimental
RFC	Royal Flying Corps
RN	Royal Navy
RNAS	Royal Naval Air Service
SE	Scouting Experimental
USAS	United States Air Service
VAD	Voluntary Aid Detachment
VC	Victoria Cross

The RFC Order of Battle
9th April 1917 Arras

3 Brigade
Brigadier General J F A Higgins DSO
HQ Albert

35 Squadron (FE2b)
Major A V Holt
Chateau de Sains

100 Squadron (FE2b)
Major M G Christie DSO MC
Le Hameau

12 (Corps) Wing
Lieutenant Colonel W G S Mitchell MC
Avesnes-le-Comte

8 Squadron (BE2)	12 Squadron (BE2)	13 Squadron (BE2)	59 Squadron (RE8)
Major E L Gossage MC	Major C S Burnett	Major E W Powell	Major R Egerton MC
Soncamp	Avesnes-le-Comte	Savy	La Bellevue

13 (Army) Wing
Lieutenant Colonel G F Pretyman DSO
Le Hameau

11 Squadron (FE2b)	29 Squadron (Nieuport)	48 Squadron (Bristol F2a)
Major C T MacLean MC	Major H V C de Cresigny MC	Major A V Bettington
Le Hameau	Le Hameau	La Bellevue

60 Squadron (Nieuport)	6 (Naval) Squadron
Major A J L Scott	Sqn Cmdr J J Petre DSC
Le Hameau	La Bellevue

3 Kite Balloon Wing
Lieutenant Colonel F H Cleaver DSO
HQ Barly

9 Kite Balloon Company	10 Kite Balloon Company	11 Kite Balloon Company	12 Kite Balloon Company
Captain G S Sansom	Major R L Farley	Captain W S Huxley	Captain E L Chute
Sections 7 and 21	Sections 5 and 28	Sections 16 and 33	Sections 35 and 36

Third Army Aircraft Park
Major R Hall
Frévent

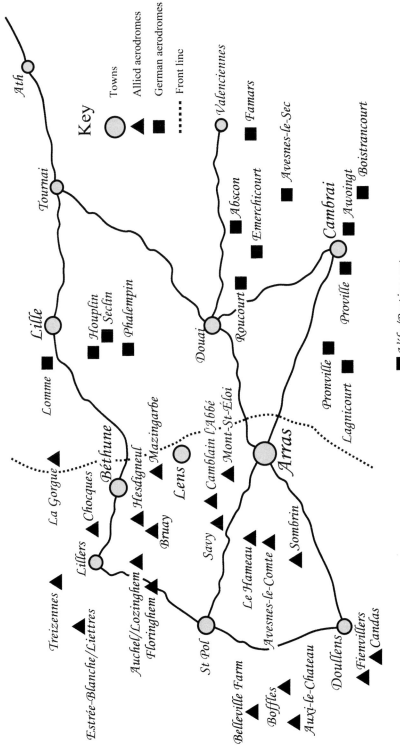

The Arras Area

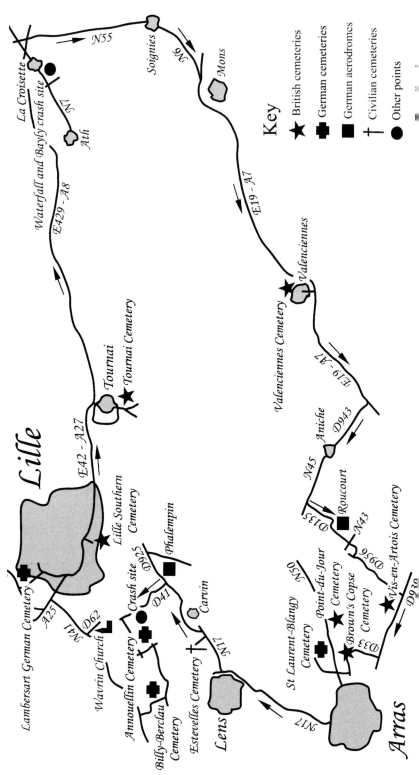

The Eastern Area

Key
- ★ British cemeteries
- ✠ German cemeteries
- ■ German aerodromes
- † Civilian cemeteries
- ● Other points

Lille

La Croisette

N55

Soignies

9N

Mons

Waterfall and Bayly crash site

N7

Ath

E429 - A8

E19 - A7

Valenciennes

Valenciennes Cemetery

E42 - A27

E19 - A7

Tournai
Tournai Cemetery

Aniche

D943

N45

Roucourt

N43

E429 - A8

Lambersart German Cemetery

A25

D62

N41

Wavrin Church

Crash site

D925

Phalempin

D41

Annœullin Cemetery

Billy-Berclau Cemetery

Carvin

N17

Estevelles Cemetery

Lens

N17

St Laurent-Blangy Cemetery

N50

Point-du-Jour Cemetery

Brown's Copse Cemetery

Vis-en-Artois Cemetery

D939

D33

D956

Arras

Chapter One

ARRAS: EASTERN AREA

This itinerary covers an area which remained in German hands for most of the war. The first part of our journey passes very close to the Canadian memorial on Vimy Ridge - perhaps the most moving and impressive Allied monument on the Western Front. On this tour the places that will be visited, together with the main points of interest, are:

Estevelles Communal Cemetery - Indra Lal Roy, Indian fighter ace
Phalempin Aerodrome - *Jasta* 30
Annouellin - Albert Ball VC crash site
Annouellin German Cemetery - Albert Ball VC
Billy-Berclau German Cemetery - Mick Mannock's last victim
Wavrin Church - Louis Bennett
Lambersart German Cemetery - Pech *Jasta* 29 and Dilthey *Jasta* 27
Lille Southern Cemetery - The first RFC night bombing casualty
Tournai Communal Cemetery, Allied Extension - Waterfall and Bayly
La Croisette - Waterfall and Bayly crash site
Valenciennes (St. Roch) Communal Cemetery - A A Callender
Roucourt Aerodrome - *Jasta* 11
Vis-en-Artois British Cemetery - Viscount Glentworth
Brown's Copse Cemetery - Major H D Harvey-Kelly, 19 Squadron
St-Laurent-Blangy German Cemetery - Kurt Schoenfelder, *Jasta* 7
Point-du-Jour Military Cemetery - C J Burke, OC 2 Wing RFC

Leave Arras on the N17 to Lens. The N17 becomes the A21. Leave at Junction 12, sign posted to Loison s/s Lens, back onto the N17. Turn left onto the D164E2 to Estevelles. Continue through the village and the cemetery is on the left.

Estevelles Communal Cemetery

There are only two Commonwealth War Graves Commission burials in this French civil cemetery and one contains the remains of the sole Indian ace of the First World War. The grave is situated in the fourth aisle from the entrance about three quarters of the way down.

Indra Lal Roy, or Laddie as he was known, was born in Calcutta on 2 December 1898. His father, a barrister, was Director of Public Prosecution in the city. Laddie left India at the age of ten and attended Colet Court

Preparatory School prior to entering St Paul's College, Kensington. He was a good athlete, captaining the school swimming team and playing in the rugby XV. He also served in the officer cadet unit for nearly three years. He had a great passion for aviation and in March 1917 left St Paul's and applied for a commission in the RFC. Unfortunately, he ran into the same prejudice that also dogged another Indian, Shri Krishna Chunda Welinkar (*Somme* page 122). Despite the fact he was well educated it was suggested that the best way for an Indian to join the RFC was as a sergeant mechanic. Laddie's brother had already served two years in France with the Honourable Artillery

Indra Lal Roy, the only Indian ace of the First World War.

Company but had not applied for a transfer to the RFC as he felt he would not get a commission.

After a direct plea to Brigadier-General Sefton Brancker, the Director of Air Organisation, Laddie joined the flying service at South Farnborough on 4 April 1917. Part of his flying training was conducted at Vendome in France, and then on 27 October of that year he joined 56 Squadron. In December he crashed his SE5 and was hospitalised, following which he returned to England. He attended the Armament School at Uxbridge and in April 1918 was graded as a technical lieutenant.

On 10 April 1918 Laddie was posted to 40 Squadron, who were operating the SE5a, though there is some doubt in what capacity - either as a pilot or a technical officer. However, a month later he was admitted to 24 General Hospital at Étaples and sent to England. He rejoined 40 Squadron on 14 June and was posted to George McElroy's flight (*Ypres* page 109). Under this great ace's tuition Laddie was to do well. His first victory was claimed on 6 July and in only thirteen days he shot down a total of ten - a remarkable achievement. Unfortunately, on 22 July his good fortune deserted him during a morning patrol. An eight-man patrol left at 0800 hours under the leadership of Captain I P R Napier, a very experienced pilot. Another of the pilots in the formation was Ben Strange (*Cambrai* page 31).

Gwilym Lewis in his SE5a D3540. (See page 115) The white sloping N was 40 Squadron's marking.

A group of *Jasta* **29 pilots. Karl Gregor is second from left. He had lost his left leg in July 1917 but returned to the unit. Fifth from the left is Harald Auffarth, who had served in two-seater units before becoming leader of** *Jasta* **29. By the end of the war he had claimed nearly 30 victories but did not receive the** *Pour le Mérite* **due to the armistice. Also in the photograph but unidentified is Bernhard Brunnecker.**

In the vicinity of Carvin they met four enemy scouts and a general fight commenced from a height of 16,000 feet. Two German fighters were claimed as crashed. One was brought down by Ben Strange and the other by Reed Landis, an American attached to the RAF. One of these claims was probably *Unteroffizier* Paul Marczinski of *Jasta* 30 who was killed and is now buried in Lambersart German Cemetery (see page 48). Landis was later awarded a British DFC and figures in another incident in this book (see page 45).

One SE5a was seen to go down in flames by an Allied anti-aircraft battery. Strange and another pilot had to land due to engine problems but Laddie failed to return. Though only one SE5a was lost a total of three were claimed and credited to pilots from *Jasta* 29 in this area at the same time, so it is difficult to decide who might have brought him down. The victorious *Jasta* 29 pilots were the commanding officer, Harald Auffarth, Karl Gregor and Bernhard Brunnecker.

In September Laddie's DFC was gazetted. Though his career was tragically short he served as an example to other Indians and showed what they were capable of given the chance. A nephew became the first Indian Air Chief.

For a fuller account of Roy's life I recommend an article by Somnath Sapru in *Cross and Cockade Great Britain,* volume five, page thirteen.

Return to the N17. Continue north east and then follow the D919 to Seclin. This becomes the D925. At the roundabout take the first right, the D62, to Phalempin. After entering Phalempin turn left into the Rue de Plouick and park. On the other side of the road is an alleyway between two houses, which gives access to the aerodrome.

Phalempin Aerodrome

The German aerodrome here was based on the farm at 85 Rue J B Lebas, which is still owned by the same family today. Some years ago the barns at the back burned down, so the rear aspect of the farm is different. There remains a First World War concrete bomb store.

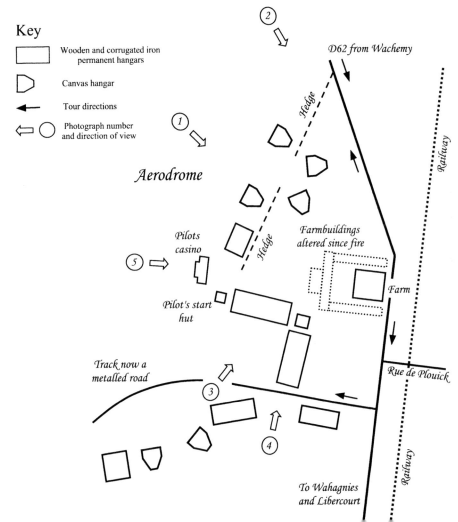

Picture No.1: Phalempin photographed during the First World War, looking southeast.

Picture No. 2: Phalempin in 2003 looking south.

On 12 August 1917 *Leutnant* Joachim von Bertrab of *Jasta* 30 took off from here and was shot down by the famous ace Edward 'Mick' Mannock (see page 113).

Jasta 30

Most German fighter units moved fairly frequently, being transferred from one part of the front to another as the situation demanded. However, *Jasta* 30 was an exception and remained here from January 1917 until August 1918. They were formed on 14 December 1916 and mobilised at Phalempin on 21 January 1917 in the 6 Armee sector and their first commander was *Oberleutnant* Hans Bethge.

Oberleutnant Hans Bethge

Bethge was born in Berlin on 6 December 1890 and served with the *BAO (Brieftauben-Abteilung-Ostende)*, a bombing unit in the Flanders

Picture No. 4: Hans Bethge, commanding officer of *Jasta* 30, on the roof of one of the wooden hangars. Rudders from captured Allied machines were mounted as wind vanes.

Hugh Welch's crashed Nieuport A6615. He is buried in Arras Road British Cemetery, Roclincourt, just north of Arras. In the background can be seen Bethge's Albatross on its nose.

area. He was posted to *KEK* Bertincourt, part of *FA* 32, on 4 August 1916 (*Cambrai* page 159) and then assigned to *Jasta* 1 on 23 August. His first claim, a BE2c of 15 Squadron, was on 29 August. After three confirmed and one unconfirmed claims, he was posted to *Jasta* 30 as its commanding officer on 14 January 1917.

At this time the area was a relatively quiet one, with the British offensive on the Somme having ground to a halt in the previous autumn.

Two months were to elapse before Bethge shot down the unit's first victory. On 28 March 1917 he brought down a Nieuport Scout of No. 1 Squadron RFC and the pilot, Second Lieutenant Hugh Welch, was killed. While landing near to his victory Bethge turned his Albatros on its nose. His score gradually mounted and on 17 August he claimed two Sopwith Camels of 8 Naval Squadron that had collided.

By March 1918 he had been awarded the Iron Cross First Class and the Knight's Cross of the Hohenzollern House Order. Following his 20th victory on 10 March he was nominated for the *Pour le Mérite*. Unfortunately, it was not approved as he was killed in action on 17 March 1918, probably during an encounter with DH4s of 57 Squadron. It could not be awarded posthumously. He was buried in Berlin.

Latter days

Command passed through a number of hands due to promotions and woundings but *Oberleutnant* Hans-Georg von der Marwitz led it for most of 1918 and was still there at the armistice. He was also the unit's second highest scoring pilot after Bethge, with approximately fifteen victories.

Jasta 30 was not one of the most successful German fighter units but

31

A concrete bomb store at Phalempin. This has now gone but there is another similar structure still remaining.

Picture No. 5: The pilot's readiness hut. Note Allied rudder on the roof.

by the end of the war had claimed 63 Allied machines for the loss of twelve pilots killed in action, five taken prisoner of war and three killed in accidents.

Return to the roundabout on the D925 and drive south west towards Carnin. In Camphin-en-Carembault turn right on the D41 to Carnin. Continue through Carnin and in the village turn right on the D41 to Annouellin. Ahead on the D41C to Allenes-les Marais. Leaving Carnin stop just beyond the Allenes-les Marais village sign after an isolated red brick house. The crash marker can be seen in the field on your left. Access is via a farm track. Avoid trampling the farmer's crops.

Albert Ball Crash Site

After the war Ball's father located the exact spot where his son had been killed and purchased the field. On the exact spot where the crash occurred he had erected two stone markers. They marked the position of the nose and the tail of the crashed SE5a. Only one stone remains and this is believed to indicate the position of the nose.

On it the visitor will see inscribed:

To the loving memory of Captain Albert Ball, VC, DSO, Two Bars, MC, Croix de Chevalier Legion d'Honneur, Order of Saint George, Russia, Hon Freeman of the City of Nottingham. One of England's Famous Airmen who fell on this spot fighting gloriously May 7th, 1917. Aged 20 years.

On the rear of the stone is carved:

This plot of land is given for the use of French soldiers by Sir Albert Ball on condition that this stone is protected.

Continue ahead to the cross roads and turn left on the D39 to Annouellin. On the right you will pass the sign to the new village school named after Albert Ball. Go left on D39 to Provin by the German cemetery sign. Left in front of the church towards Carnin and then left at German sign for the cemetery.

The marker at Ball's crash site.

33

Annoeullin German Cemetery

By German standards this is a small cemetery with only 1,627 graves but it contains one burial of particular interest to the British visitor.

The grave we are visiting is that of one of Britain's first popular flying heroes, Albert Ball. His grave is unusual as it is the sole British one in a German cemetery and has a civilian headstone, not having been replaced with a Commonwealth War Graves Commission one. It is on the right side of the cemetery towards the back.

Albert Ball VC

Ball was born in Nottingham on 14 August 1896 into a well-off family. His father, also Albert, was engaged in local politics and served four terms as the Mayor of Nottingham, being knighted for his public service in 1924. The young Albert had a happy childhood and was fascinated by all things mechanical. In 1913 he left Trent College and busied himself with the Universal Engineering Works in Nottingham.

When war was declared a little over a year later he joined the 2/7 Sherwood Foresters. In late 1915 he paid for his own flying tuition with the Ruffy Baumann School at Hendon (now the site of the Royal Air Force Museum) and then transferred to the RFC. After further service training he was posted to No. 22 Squadron at Gosport in January 1916.

During February he received his first operational posting and arrived at 13 Squadron, who were based at Marieux, southeast of Doullens. They were equipped with the ubiquitous two-seater BE2, which Ball flew on artillery observation and reconnaissance. However, they also had a single-seat Bristol Scout, which was fitted with a forward firing machine gun for scouting duties, and Ball claimed one victory in this type of machine.

On 7 May 1916 Ball transferred to 11 Squadron on the other side of the same aerodrome at Savy, having been recommended as a single-seat pilot. Here he encountered the French Nieuport Scout in which he was to establish his reputation as the RFC's leading fighter pilot. His first claims on this machine occurred on 29 May when two German aeroplanes were forced to land. At the end of June he was notified that he had been awarded the Military Cross, having brought down five enemy machines.

In the middle of July Ball, who was feeling fatigued, asked his squadron commander if it would be possible to have a few days rest. Unfortunately his request backfired as he found himself sent to 8 Squadron flying BE2s again! After a month flying two-seaters he was re-posted to 11 Squadron where he took over a brand new Nieuport Scout. On 22 August Ball made three claims in one day, the first time this feat had been achieved in the RFC (*Cambrai* page 84).

Near the end of August Ball was posted to 60 Squadron which was being re-equipped as a scout squadron and he took his Nieuport with him. His aggressive tactics earned a DSO at the beginning of September, shortly before he went on leave, after seventeen victories. It was during this leave that he first experienced some of the fame and adulation that was to embarrass him.

At the beginning of October Ball was posted to Home Establishment. He had claimed 32 enemy machines, attacking any odds at any time and had provided a splendid example to the RFC for courage and aggression. At home he was feted by all and sundry and pursued by the Press. On 18 November 1916 he attended an investiture at Buckingham Palace and received his DSO with two bars plus his MC. He was the first person in the British army to receive three DSOs. On February 19 1917 at a large function Ball was made an Honorary Freeman of the City of Nottingham, a rare distinction for someone so young.

Ball was given a number of mundane jobs or postings which dissatisfied him, as they were ill-suited to his talents. He lobbied for a return to France without success until in February he was notified

Albert Ball, Britain's first flying hero. Taken in front of a Nieuport Scout when serving with 60 Squadron.

of a posting to 56 Squadron, who were working up for action in France. He was placed in command of A Flight. The squadron was due to be the first unit to take the new Royal Aircraft Factory SE5 to France.

James McCudden, the great fighter pilot, described the machine thus:

The SE5 which I was now flying was a most efficient fighting machine, far and away superior to the enemy machines of that period. It had a Vickers' gun, shooting forward through the propeller, and a Lewis gun shooting forward over the top plane, parallel to the Vickers', but above the propeller. The pilot could also incline the Lewis gun upwards in such a way that he could shoot vertically upwards at a target that presented itself. As a matter of fact, these guns were rarely used in this manner, as it was quite a work of art to pull this gun down and shoot upwards, and at the same time manage one's machine accurately. The idea of using a Lewis gun on the top plane of an S.E. was first put forward by the

35

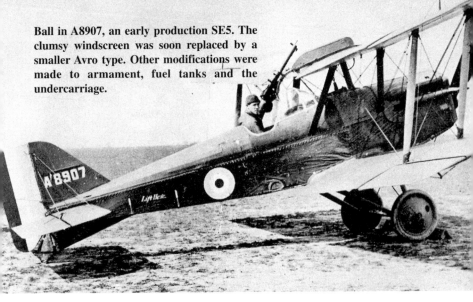

Ball in A8907, an early production SE5. The clumsy windscreen was soon replaced by a smaller Avro type. Other modifications were made to armament, fuel tanks and the undercarriage.

late Captain Ball, who used his top gun with such excellent success in another Squadron whilst flying Nieuports.

Other good points of the S.E. were its great strength, its diving and zooming powers, and its splendid view. Apart from this, it was a most warm, comfortable and easy machine to fly.

It was very fine to be on a machine that was faster than the Huns, and I may say that it increased one's confidence enormously to know that one could run away just as soon as things became too hot for one.

Ball had taken a dislike to the SE5 on a short acquaintance the previous November and shortly after 56 Squadron arrived on the Western Front he was unusually allocated a Nieuport Scout for his personal use. Flying this machine Ball claimed the squadron's first victory when he sent an Albatros two-seater down to crash on 6 May 1917.

In time Ball was won over to the advantages of the SE5, particularly as it had two machine guns and was a steadier gun platform.

On 6 May Ball claimed his 44th and last victim, an Albatros DIII, whilst flying his Nieuport Scout. The following day he was killed leading a patrol of eleven machines. An account of this action appears in *Somme* page 55.

At the end of his fuel Ball's machine came out of cloud and crashed at Annoeullin, well behind the German front line. His only injuries were those caused by the crash. As with a lot of the First World War flying casualties his end remains a mystery. Tired after a long patrol he probably became disorientated in cloud and lost control at too low an altitude to recover.

He was buried with full military honours by the Germans and the

Nieuport Scout B1522 in which Ball scored 56 Squadron's first victory and his own last victory on 6 May 1917. It later served for short periods in 1 and 29 Squadrons before being damaged in a crash. Here it is shown with a training unit in Egypt during 1918.

funeral was attended by a number of British prisoners of war.

On 8 June 1917 the London Gazette carried the announcement of a posthumous Victoria Cross to Ball. The citation reads:

For most conspicuous and consistent bravery from the 25th of April to the 6th of May 1917, during which period Captain Ball took part in twenty-six combats in the air and destroyed eleven hostile aeroplanes, drove down two out of control, and forced several others to land. In these combats Captain Ball, flying alone, on one occasion fought six hostile machines, twice he fought five, and once

A message dropped by the Germans confirming the death of Albert Ball.

> An das
>
> R. F. C.
>
> Capitain **B a l l** am 7.5.17 im Luft=
> kampf mit ebenbürtigem Gegner gefallen.
> Er wurde in A n m o e u l l i n beerdigt.
> Nachtrag: Leutnant French am 20.5.17 durch
> Abwehrfeuer zum Absturz gebracht; unverwundet
> in Gefangenschaft geraten.

four. When leading two other British aeroplanes he attacked an enemy formation of eight. On each of these occasions he brought down at least one enemy. Several times his aeroplane was badly damaged, once so seriously that but for the most delicate handling his machine would have collapsed, as nearly all the control wires had been shot away. On returning with a damaged machine he had always to be restrained from immediately going out in another.

In all, Captain Ball has destroyed forty-three German aeroplanes and one balloon, and has always displayed most exceptional courage, determination and skill.

Ball epitomised the lone hunter, attacking regardless of odds and was an inspiration to his fellow fliers and a hero to his countrymen. Today he occupies an honoured grave surrounded by his former adversaries.

For an excellent account of Ball's life I recommend *Albert Ball, VC* by Chaz Bowyer (see Further Reading).

Return to the D39 and turn left to Provin. Continue through the village and after the level crossing pick up signs ahead for Billy-Berclau. Pass over the canal to the roundabout and follow signs to Centre Ville. After the town centre, pass the church and follow German signs to the cemetery.

Billy-Berclau German Cemetery

It is sad to say that the first time I visited this cemetery about two thirds of the metal crosses had been snapped off just above the ground in a mindless act of vandalism. The cemetery staff had been forced to drive the broken ends into the grass to stand them up again. There are a number of memorials to infantry regiments and a red stone pillar in the centre. The two graves (7/321, 7/331) we are visiting are in the top far left corner in a side extension and are in the very back row.

Mick Mannock's last victory

We are hear to pay our respects to two German aviators, *Vizefeldwebel* Josef Hein and *Leutnant* Ludwig Schöpf of *FA(A)* 292 who are connected with arguably the greatest British and Empire ace of the First World War, Edward 'Mick' Mannock. They were his 61st and last victory.

In *Airfields and Airmen Ypres* page 106, there is an account of Mannock's career. By late July 1918, after service in 40 and 74 Squadrons and now in command of 85 Squadron, he had 60 official victories. His total was second only to the Canadian ace Billy Bishop, whom he had replaced as commander of 85 Squadron (see page 142). The style of the two could not have been more different. Bishop had continued his lone wolf tactics and the squadron had been largely left to its own devices. But

Pilots of 74 Squadron before leaving for France. On the left is Mick Mannock and to his left is Major Keith 'Grid' Caldwell, the commanding officer. Seated on the right is W E Young, who later commanded No. 1 Squadron and figures in an incident on page 181.

Mannock promoted teamwork and soon welded the unit into an efficient one. He was held in enormous esteem by all members of the squadron and throughout the RFC/RAF.

One of the new members of the squadron was D C Inglis:

The rest of the pilots and most of the mechanics of the Squadron were deep in their slumbers as their leader walked across the dewy grass to his machine for the last time. The first streak of dawn was lighting the horizon. The birds wakening with the dawn were singing their chorus with crisp vigour. Mannock drew his companion's attention to a particular blackbird which appeared to be leading the others. "Do you hear that bird?" he said to Inglis. "He is like me. He is full of the joy of life. He is wishing us luck."

In the July 1938 edition of the aviation magazine *Popular Flying*, exactly twenty years after the event, Inglis wrote an account of the last flight on 26 July 1918 under the pseudonym of 'Kiwi':

I considered myself fortunate indeed to be in 85 Squadron under Major Mannock's command.

The Major did not seek glory for himself alone, but on frequent

39

The aircrew of 85 Squadron at St Omer on 21 June 1918, the day Mick Mannock was promoted to major and appointed to command of the unit, instead of Billy Bishop. Donald Inglis is on the extreme right.

occasions gave away "Huns" to new pilots, as happened in my case.

"Have you got a Hun yet, Kiwi?" He asked me one day.

Upon my replying in the negative he said in his matter-of-fact way, "Well, we'll go out and get one."

"Mick's" usual method when taking a man out to get a "Hun" was to go last thing in the evening or at dawn, as the "Hun" two-seaters came over our side after we left at night or before we arrived in the morning. To enable him to surprise them he would keep right down on the carpet, and when he spotted a "Hun" he would turn for home, climbing full out, then with a sudden half roll and a dive, cut the "Hun" off and attack him from in front and at an angle as he tried to get home.

Our machines had been previously warmed up, and we climbed aboard to take off. "Mick" set off all right, but as I went to do likewise I discovered to my chagrin my tail plane control was jammed. Naturally, I did not use the King's English as I called the mechanic's aid - but although they worked hard on the machine, nothing would free the control. By this time the Major's machine had vanished from sight. This was the first time he had ever gone out alone whilst with us, and anxiously I paced up and down the tarmac awaiting my Commander's return.

At last I heard the welcome purr of his plane and a great sense of relief swept over me as he landed safe and sound. Rushing over to him I blurted out the cause of my delay. He merely grinned and replied calmly,"That's all right, Kiwi! We'll go out in the morning and get one."

That was all! He was never one to waste words.

I cannot quite recollect now what happened, but through a misunderstanding the Major and I did not leave at dawn according to schedule.

"Sit close on my tail, and if you get too far away I will waggle my wings!" were the Major's brief instructions to me

You will understand that as "Mick" Mannock was not flying above 50 feet - and moreover never in a straight line for more than a few seconds - if one dropped behind more than about 25 feet his wings waggled and so it was impossible to see anything but the tail of the plane.

I followed him as directed along the front between Nieppe Forest and Mont Kimmell (sic), where he kept mostly to the gullies, when he suddenly turned for home and commenced climbing full out. I knew from this he must have spotted a "Hun".

As I climbed after "Mick" I kept my eyes skinned for the "Hun", but could not pick him up. However, a few moments later I noticed that Mannock half-rolled and went into a power dive. But the "Hun" must have spotted "Mick" as he was attacking from the rear. Apparently he disabled the rear gunner, as when I attacked the "Hun" gunner was not shooting.

Both my guns were going full out, when suddenly the "Hun's" tail shot up in front of me. A chill ran through me as I pulled up, just missing his tail and wing by a fraction. Looking back I saw my first "Hun" going down in a mass of flames.

We circled once and started for home. The realisation came to me we were being shot at from the ground when I saw the Major was kicking his rudder. Suddenly a small flame appeared on the right side of "Mick's" machine, and simultaneously he stopped kicking his rudder. The plane went into a slow right-hand turn, the flame growing in intensity, and as the machine hit the ground it burst into a mass of flame.

I circled at about 20 feet hoping for the best - but Mannock had made his last flight.

Inglis' machine was badly hit by ground fire and his engine failed after the fuel tank was hit. He was just able to land on the British side of the front line. Despite the almost matter-of-fact last line in the above account, in fact Inglis was deeply affected by Mannock's loss and was to remain so for the rest of life. He recalled in Taffy Jones' book on Mannock, *King of Air Fighters*:

A Junkers CL1. Being an all metal cantilever wing monoplane, it was an advanced design.

> *"Poor old Mick", all I could say when I got into the trench was
> that the bloody bastards had shot my Major down in flames.*

Mannock's body was never recovered though his personal possessions were returned to the family after the war from Germany. His name is recorded on the Air Forces Memorial to the Missing at Arras. For an account of the search for his grave see *Airfields and Airmen: The Channel Coast,* Chapter Three, Pacaut.

Due to the lack of German records it has not been possible to ascertain the type of machine that Schopf and Hein were flying, though it has been assumed it was a DFW. In recent years it has also been suggested it was a Junkers CL1, which was basically a two-seater version of the Junkers J9 or D1. The type was a low-wing metal-skinned monoplane, of which the first were introduced in mid-1918, but less than 50 had been delivered by the end of the war. An unusual machine as this would surely have warranted comment from Inglis, though he only describes it in his combat report as a *Two-seater. Type unknown.*

Donald Clyde Inglis

Born on 22 June 1893, he was a motor engineer in Christchurch, New Zealand, when war was declared. After joining the New Zealand field artillery as a bombardier-fitter, he earned a DCM in Gallipoli for repairing three guns under heavy enemy fire. Joining the RFC in late summer 1917 Inglis learned to fly with 85 Squadron. He attended gunnery school and returned to 85 in time to travel with them to France on 22 May 1918, under the leadership of the legendary Billy Bishop, as mentioned earlier. After the Mannock incident Inglis only claimed one more victory, a Fokker DVII destroyed on 9 October. He remained with 85 Squadron until 15 December 1918, returning to Home Establishment and was demobilised in July 1919.

Continue ahead as it is a one-way street. Turn right at the Stop sign. Pick up the blue A25 motorway signs to Lille, then on to the N47. Turn right on the N41 to Lille. Right on the D62 to Beachamps-Ligny. Right at the roundabout to Wavrin. Over the level crossing and follow the one-way system to the church.

Wavrin Church

We are visiting the church to view a memorial erected by the local people to commemorate a United States pilot serving in an RAF squadron who was killed near here.

It took a number of visits before we were able to find someone who could unlock the church for us and even then the plaque was hidden by the props used in a children's play.

The plaque on the wall in the church at Wavrin. Note the incorrect spelling of Bennett.

Louis Bennett Jnr

The reader will be aware from the other books in this series that a large number of US pilots served in the British flying services during the Great War. Some had enlisted before the United States entered the war, whilst others were on secondment to gain experience before joining USAS units. Many were killed and a fair number earned British gallantry awards. One of these, who had a meteoric career, was Louis Bennett Jnr.

Bennett was born on 22 September 1894 in Weston, West Virginia and studied at Yale from 1913 until 1917, when he joined the RFC in Toronto. After initial training he was sent overseas and arrived in England on 25 February 1918. After training at No. 2 School of Aerial Gunnery and with 90 Squadron he was posted to France on 20 July. After two days in No. 1 Aeroplane Supply Depot Pool he was posted to

Louis Bennett Jnr. This picture was taken during training.

Am 22. Aug. in Marquillies herunter gesch. engl. Flieger.

This is reputed to be the wreckage of Bennett's machine. The location is correct but the date is not.

40 Squadron RAF flying SE5as. Here he joined the redoubtable Irish ace George McElroy's C Flight (*Ypres* page 109).

Following a short settling-in period he claimed his first victim on 15 August, shooting down a Fokker DVII out of control. He then scored at a phenomenal rate. On 17th he claimed a balloon and a two-seater, on 19th four balloons and on 22nd two balloons. He had a penchant for enemy observation balloons, considered by many to be too dangerous a target. Nine of these fell to Bennett's gun but they would ultimately be his

The German balloon attacked by Louis Bennett.

The observer, Emil Merkelbach, standing next to the basket of his balloon.

undoing.

On 8 August, Ludendorff's 'Black Day', the Allies had started their great offensive against the Germans, which was to end the war. The flying services were heavily committed to supporting the army, involving ground attack - always a dangerous task. On 24 August Bennett left at midday on an offensive patrol and bombing mission. One of the other 40 Squadron pilots engaged on this operation was another American pilot, Reed Landis, whom we met on page 27. Bennett was seen to shoot down two balloons and then attack a third but was brought down by ground fire. His machine burst into flames and he jumped before it hit the ground, dying of his injuries.

His victories had been claimed in such a short time, an amazing thirteen in only ten days, that there had not been a chance to recommend him for an award, though he was Mentioned in Despatches on 16 March 1919. This was the only award, apart from the Victoria Cross, which could be given posthumously.

There was much confusion as to where he had been buried. The RAF was always reluctant to inform relatives of the fates or burial places of their loved ones unless they had definite confirmation. GHQ reported to the Air Ministry, after an enquiry from Bennett's mother, that he had died in Wavre Hospital and been buried in the local cemetery. In February 1919, after a direct enquiry, the German Red Cross confirmed he was buried in grave 590 of Wavrin civilian cemetery, a few kilometres south west of Lille. Again there is some confusion as he is reported to have been buried in the

German cemetery at Wavrin.

After the war Bennett's mother had several memorials erected in memory of her son. The church in Wavrin was re-built with funds donated by Mrs Bennett and today is the village hall. She also financed the Flying Corps stained glass memorial window in the Great Nave of Westminster Abbey, which was unveiled on 26 May 1922.

Following the Armistice Louis Bennett's body was transferred to the United States and on 14 April 1920 was re-interred in the family plot at Weston, West Virginia.

Return to the N41 and continue towards Lille. Follow A25 to Armentières and Dunkirk, then Tourcoing and Gaud signs on to the N352. At Junction 7 turn right onto the D257 to Lambersart. At the first traffic lights turn left to Les Conquerants into Rue Monge. At the T junction left again and continue to the cemetery on the left.

Lambersart German Cemetery

This cemetery contains only First World War casualties and there are a total of 4,689. It is divided in three plots, numbered from left to right, and has a very large cross in the centre. There are a number of aviators here of which three are of particular interest. The first one, Helmuth Dilthey, is in Plot I, in the centre, abeam the large cross.

Helmuth Dilthey (1/1162)
Dilthey was born at Rheydt, near Dusseldorf, on 9 February 1894. After joining the flying service in November 1914 he served on the Eastern Front from the summer of 1915 with a two-seater unit, *FA* 50. By late 1916 he had been awarded both classes of the Iron Cross and was commissioned. After pilot training at *Jastaschule* in the spring of 1917, he

The pilots of *Jasta* 27. Hermann Göring, the staffel leader, is eighth from the right and Dilthey sixth from the right.

Helmut Dilthey with his Albatros DVa. The Saxon colours, green and white, were the early *Jasta* 40 marking.

was posted to *Jasta* 27, commanded by Hermann Göring, on 19 May. Dilthey's first claim was on 24 July when he brought down a Sopwith Triplane from 10 Naval Squadron. The pilot, Flight Sub Lieutenant T C May, a Canadian from Toronto, was killed and has no known grave.

Dilthey scored steadily and by February 1918 had claimed a total of six. On 14 April 1918 he was posted to command *Jasta* 40, down on the French front. His second-in-command was Carl Degelow, who wrote in his autobiography, *Germany's Last Knight of the Air*:

> The rate of attrition among German combat pilots rose steadily. To keep the frontline squadrons up to a reasonable level of success, only men with proven combat records were given positions of command. Amongst the Jagdstaffeln this meant that virtually any pilot who shot down five enemy aircraft could count on becoming either the commanding officer or at least the second in command of a frontline Staffel. Non-commissioned officers and other ranks were rapidly promoted to commissioned status (although always in the Reserves, never the Regular Army) if their victory scores were impressive enough, as it was proven that tenacity in the air was a better quality of leadership than formal education and 'class' background. As there were ultimately 81 German Staffeln, the need for such an expedient becomes obvious.

Jasta 40, a Saxon unit, was formed on 15 August 1917. On 6 April 1918 they were transferred to 4 *Armee* front, opposite the British and Belgians, and a little over a week later Dilthey arrived as commanding officer. They were operating a mix of Pfalz DIIIs and Albatros DVas. During their time on the French sector they had only claimed four enemy machines but lost two pilots killed. Dilthey was obviously brought in to breathe new life into the unit.

On 5 June he claimed his seventh victim, a British kite balloon. A month later disaster struck when the *jasta* attacked a formation of British

DH4 bombers. Ten machines from 107 Squadron had taken off to attack targets in the Lille area. Second Class Air Mechanic James Page Hazell, the gunner with Second Lieutenant John Roberts Brown, described the action in his combat report:

> *Just before releasing bombs over Lille, 3 E.A. attacked the Formation in rear. 1 E.A. dived on rear right machine. I fired 40 rounds at this E.A. at about 150 yards range. The E.A. burst into flames immediately and I last saw it about 4,000 feet below still in flames.*

Dilthey, though equipped with a parachute, was killed and it was thought within the *jasta* that he had been hit by German anti-aircraft fire and this had cut his parachute lines.

Degelow took over command of *Jasta* 40 and, after being re-equipped with superior machines, turned it into a more effective unit. He ended the war with 30 victories and the *Pour le Mérite*. He died on 9 November 1970 in Hamburg.

J R Brown, born on 11 May 1896, had joined the RFC, initially in the ranks but had been quickly commissioned, in the summer of 1917, having been an accountant with a shipbuilding company in Jarrow-on-Tyne. After pilot training he had arrived at 107 Squadron on 7 June 1918. Hospitalised three days after the Dilthey incident, he left the squadron in September. He served in the RAF again during the Second World War and died on 14 July 1972.

J P Hazell was born on 26 August 1899 in Grimsby and in civil life had been a driver. He served in the Royal Navy from September 1917 until January 1918, as an ordinary seaman, before transferring to the RNAS. Joining 107 Squadron in May 1918, he was temporarily hospitalised later in July due to a wound and returned to England in March 1919 with the squadron cadre. He was still with them when the unit was disbanded on 13 August 1919 and was demobilized in January 1920. Shortly before he left the service he received the French *Croix de Guerre avec Etoile en Vermeuil*.

Paul Marczinski (2/723)

The next grave we are visiting is in the right centre of Plot II, again abeam the large cross. Little is known about him other than he was born on 18 May 1898 in Lyck. After *Jastaschule* he was posted to *Jasta* 30 on 5 May 1918. Just two months later he was killed in action, near Point Maudit, by a pilot from 40 Squadron. It was during this engagement that Indra Lal Roy was killed and though Ben Strange appears to have been given credit it would seem more likely that an American pilot serving with 40 Squadron, Reed Landis, was the probable victor. For more information regarding this action see page 27.

Karl Pech (2/1230)

The last grave we are visiting is that of Karl Pech which is at the rear of Plot II. He was born on 9 December 1894 in Seidau. Joining *Jasta* 29 on 18 February 1918 from *Jastaschule* as a *flieger* he was promoted to *unteroffizier* on 20 March and then *vizefeldwebel*. His first claim was on 13 March, a DH4. His last victories were on 18 May when he brought down two Sopwith Camels of 210 Squadron (previously 10 Naval Squadron), making a total of nine.

On 19 May 1918 *Jasta* 29 encountered an eight-man Offensive Patrol from 29 Squadron led by a very experienced flight commander, Captain H G White. What occurred is described in a recommendation for an immediate award by the commanding officer of 29 Squadron, Major C H Dixon:

> *Capt White was leading a patrol at 6,000 ft east of Bailleul and encountered 9 hostile scouts. Three of his patrol were driven west, practically immediately, and Capt White was left alone. He dived on one of the EA and fired about 100 rounds at very close range. The EA 'zoomed' to the left and its top plane caught the leading edge of Capt White's machine, causing the EA to turn a cartwheel over his (Capt White's) machine. The shock of the collision flung Capt White forward on to the gun mounting, and stopped his engine. The EA went down into a dive and Capt White - expecting his machine to break up at any moment dived after it - firing about 100 rounds.*
>
> *The right wing of the EA fell off, and it went down completely out of control. Capt White then turned round, and turned west to endeavour to recross the lines. He was followed back by 5 EA scouts for some distance until these were driven off by friendly machines. Capt White managed to keep his machine fairly straight by putting on hard left bank, left rudder and leaning over the side of the cockpit. Near the ground the machine became uncontrollable and it crashed on landing near Eecke. The centre section wings of the*

Karl Pech of *Jasta* 29 in front of his Pfalz DIII.

machine were broken, and the right hand planes had anhedral instead of dihedral. The right hand top plane was badly damaged but the main spars held. The fabric was completely torn off.

Hugh Granville White

Hugh White was born on 1 March 1898 in Maidstone and entered the Royal Military College, Sandhurst when he was seventeen. Attached to the RFC he joined 20 Squadron flying FE2s. Here he was known as the 'Child Pilot' due to his age. He completed nearly a year's service in this unit, reaching the position of flight commander, having claimed three enemy machines, one of which came down in Allied lines and was captured.

After training appointments in England, he returned to France during February 1918 as a flight commander in 29 Squadron, initially flying Nieuport scouts, then SE5as. Pech was his last claim and on 22 May he was posted home for a rest.

White's experience epitomises the unfairness of the honours and awards system. Having spent a gruelling year in 20 Squadron flying FE2s, including bringing down three enemy machines, he then claimed a further four victories and avoided a near fatal collision in 29 Squadron. He finished the war without a gallantry award of any kind.

Hugh White (left) when an instructor at Yatesbury. By a quirk of fate a 29 Squadron pilot brought down a *Jasta* 29 pilot.

Granted an RAF permanent commission in 1919, White retired in 1955 as an Air Vice-Marshal, having received a CB and a CBE. He died on 23 September 1983.

Return to the D257, then turn left going south into Lille. Pass over two canals then go right following Toutes Directions. Go ahead onto the motorway A25 towards Paris. At Junction 3 follow signs to Wattignies. Continue ahead and the cemetery entrance is on the left.

Lille Southern Cemetery

The grave (III A29) we have come to visit in this cemetery (16/3), Lieutenant A St J M Warrand, concerns the first attempt by the RFC to bomb at night.

Walk down the centre aisle until the circle and take the path between the white stones marked M2 and N2. Continue along and the British Plot III is on the left. From the entrance the grave is in the far left corner against the hedge. Like most French civilian cemeteries there are opening hours, which vary with time of year but are approximately 0800 to 1645 hours.

Lille was occupied by the Germans from October 1914 until October 1918. The Southern Cemetery was used by them for most of the war and after the Armistice by the 39th Stationary Hospital and the 1st Australian CCS. It was employed again in 1940 and now commemorates 600 First World War, plus 300 Second World War casualties.

The first night bombing by the RFC (III A29)

G W Mapplebeck.

In *Somme* page 44 there is a description of the first historic reconnaissance by the RFC, involving Lieutenants G W Mapplebeck and P B Joubert, which occurred on 19 August 1914.

Gilbert Mapplebeck was also involved in the first night bombing operation that was mounted on the night of 10/11 March 1915 and involved three pilots of 4 Squadron. The other two pilots were Captain R G Barton and Lieutenant A St J Warrand. They left St Omer and landed at Bailleul at 1625 hours, in order to be closer to their target. Here the bombs were fitted (*Ypres* page 69). Each machine carried two 100-lb bombs mounted on carriers designed and built in the squadron. In addition the cockpits had been fitted with electric lights in order to read the maps and instruments. Two signalling lights were placed on the ground five miles apart aligned on the objective to guide the bombers. This operation required considerable skill and courage, as there was little in the way of navigation aids and no instruments for blind flying. Shortly after take off Barton crashed, wrecking his machine. Mapplebeck later recalled:

Started for Lille, Barton, Warrand, Map. Night was pitch dark and rather foggy. I lost sight of the others almost immediately and saw nothing from 800 - 1000 feet. The machine twice got out of control. I flew on for five minutes, engine going badly and making horrid noises, so I turned back and landed. The bombs fortunately not exploding. Found that the engine cover was touching the flywheel. Ran the engine on the ground, and, as it appeared all right, started out again without making any alteration. Flew on compass for 25 minutes and began to be shot at furiously. Bullets going through planes and fuselage just in front of me. Two of them hit one of my fingers in almost the same place, but only making scratches. A few minutes later I knew I must be over Lille, so I flew round intending to wait about until the weather cleared sufficiently to allow me to see my target. The next moment I was fired at more furiously than ever, bullets zipping through all parts of the machine. Then the engine stopped. Not as though through lack of oil (which would have been the case had the sump been smashed), but as if the petrol pipe or magneto had been hit "At last!" I thought "I am for it." I did not think I should be alive after landing and the least I expected was to be made prisoner. On thinking over the cause of engine stoppage since, I have come to the conclusion that both petrol tanks must have been hit. For I remember hearing two or three particularly big thuds in front of me above the rattle of the others. The Huns afterwards found the tanks empty.

I commenced to plane down. I knew that I must be just by Lille, and that there must be buildings all around, and in all probability chimneys. When my engine stopped I was at about 1200 or 1500 feet. I glided down to 150 feet without seeing the ground, even when I did so, it was only the ground directly underneath me. Here I saw two or three groups of buildings in the middle of which was a ploughed field. I turned the machine into it, and landed without breaking anything, though she tried to turn over on her nose. I immediately undid my belt, and prepared to get out, intending to burn the machine by shooting a hole in the tank, and then firing the pistol into the petrol. (As it happened this would have been of no use, as the tanks were found to be empty by the Huns.) At this moment I heard a voice not far away, and on turning round I saw figures, with what appeared to be rifles in their hands, about 30 yards away running towards the machine. So, guessing these to be "Uhlans" or some other kind of land-Hun, I thought discretion to be the better part of valour, and proceeded to quit. Knowing that the first place they were sure to hunt for me would be the buildings in the vicinity of the machine, I dodged round the corner of a big brick shed and then made straight away for the open country. This apparently put them right off my track as no one followed.

Details of Mapplebeck's career and subsequent fate are described after the following section concerning Warrand.

52

Be2a No.487 in which G W Mapplebeck failed to return on 11 March 1915. Though a two-seater machine it was being flown solo during this operation.

Alastair St John Munro Warrand (III A29)

Warrand was born on 12 January 1889 at Polmont in Stirlingshire. His father, though a steel roof and bridge builder, described his profession as a gentleman at large. After attending King's School, Canterbury, Warrand applied for the RMA or RMC in April 1906 and was commissioned into the Black Watch on 9 October 1907. From April 1912 until August 1914 he was seconded to the West African Field Force. He learned to fly at his own expense with the Vickers School at Brooklands, gaining his Royal Aero Club certificate, No. 840, in July 1914. On 21 October he was gazetted as a flying officer in the RFC.

After take off from Bailleul at 0445 hours on the morning of 11 March 1915, Warrand is known to have flown over the first guiding light and twenty minutes later two explosions were heard. He was brought into Lille two days later with a gun shot wound to the lower part of his right leg, though Mapplebeck believed it may have been broken in the

A St J Warrand.

landing. The German surgeons decided not to amputate the gangrenous leg but late on 18 March they changed their minds and the operation was scheduled for the following morning. Unfortunately, at 0300 hours Warrand died of his injuries. A British nurse, Miss C D M Bellamy, was with him when he passed away. The funeral was conducted by the Reverend D F K Moore, the former pastor of St James' Hill.

Gilbert William Mapplebeck

Mapplebeck was born on 26 August 1892 in Liverpool and was commissioned into the King's Liverpool Regiment. He gained his Royal Aero Club certificate in January 1913 at the Deperdussin School, Hendon. In June he was seriously injured in a flying accident at CFS when, after a bad landing, he had been thrown out and suffered a fractured skull. He went out to France with the BEF in August 1914 but was seriously injured again on 22 September 1914 with wounds to the thigh and abdomen. After discharge from hospital he was posted to 4 Squadron.

After his landing Mapplebeck hid in an empty house and then was taken to Lille by friendly French who looked after him. The Germans were desperate to apprehend him and notices were posted offering a reward for his capture and threatening death to anyone who helped him. Eventually his escape was organised and he walked into Holland and was back in England by the middle of April.

Unfortunately, a number of civilians were implicated in Mapplebeck's escape, of whom four were sentenced to death and several others to imprisonment. In September 1921 a diary written by Mapplebeck while he was hiding was handed into the Air Ministry by a British officer. It had been given to him by a German waiter in Berlin who had found it hidden in a chair in a house in Lille. It was presumed that this man had been working in an orderly room or in intelligence. Included with the paperwork was a list of the civilians involved and their sentences.

Mapplebeck was killed in a flying accident in a Morane on 24 August 1915 and is buried in Streatham Cemetery, London. His brother Tom also served in the RFC and was taken prisoner (*Cambrai*, page 37).

Return to the roundabout and follow motorway signs to Valenciennes and Brussels. Continue to follow Brussels onto the A27-E42, until you turn off at Junction 34 to Tournai. At roundabout turn right onto the ring road to Douai. In 200 yards turn left at the green War Graves Commission sign to the cemetery on the right.

Tournai Communal Cemetery, Allied Extension

Tournai was captured by the German II Corps on 23 August 1914 and was not recaptured by the Allies until 8 November 1918. The cemetery (17/3) was used by the Germans to bury their dead and prisoners of war. The 818 Commonwealth burials include approximately 50 from the retreat of the BEF in 1940. This is a civil cemetery and is open from 0800 to 1745 hours each day, including Saturdays and Sundays. The two graves we have come to pay our respects to (III G3 and III G4) were the first operational losses suffered by the RFC and are in the front row to the left of the centre aisle near the Stone of Remembrance.

Second Lieutenant Vincent Waterfall (III G4)

In *Airfields and Airmen, Cambrai,* page 42, in the section concerning the aerodrome at Maubeuge, the early operational history of the RFC was described, including the first casualties. A number of aircrew had been killed after the outbreak of war, but these had been the result of accidents.

On 22 August 1914 the RFC lost its first machine in action, when Avro No. 390 of 5 Squadron, crewed by Second Lieutenants V Waterfall and C G G Bayly, failed to return. They took off at 1016 hours on a reconnaissance and were reported missing the following day. It was their loss that probably gave the Germans the first indication of the presence of British forces.

Waterfall was born on 25 May 1891 in Grimsby and was gazetted into the 3rd Battalion East Yorkshire Regiment in January 1912. In the 23 September 1914 edition of the popular aviation weekly magazine, *The Aeroplane*, there was the following:

Vincent Waterfall.

The relatives of Lieutenant Vincent Waterfall, R.F.C., have been informed by the War Office that his body and that of his observer, Lieut. C. G. Bayly, were found by a Belgian at some place not stated, and were hidden so that they should not be found by the Germans.

Mr. Waterfall will be remembered by many at Brooklands as a very promising pilot. He took his certificate No. 461 at the Vickers School on April 22nd, 1913, and afterwards flew on various machines, particularly doing some good flying on the Martin-Handasyde aeroplane. Personally he was a fine specimen of the best type of English public school boy, and had the makings of an officer of the very best class. His high spirits, which were absolutely without harm to anybody, and his unfailing good nature, endeared him to all who knew him, and he will be greatly missed and deeply regretted by his many friends, who will join in tendering to the lady to whom he was engaged and to his relatives their deepest sympathy. Mr. Waterfall joined the Flying Corps direct in July for a course of instruction at Farnborough, and was gazetted a Flying Officer on August 24th, with date of August 5th.

Charles George Gordon Bayly (III G3)

Though Bayly was flying as observer to Waterfall he was himself a qualified pilot, having gained his 'ticket', No. 441, on 18 March 1913.

C G G Bayly.

Bayly was born on 30 May 1891 at Rondebosch, Cape Colony, South Africa. He came from a military family, his great uncle was General Gordon of Khartoum, while his uncle was Admiral Sir Lewis Bayly. After Diocesan College in Rondebosch, he continued his education in England and entered the Royal Military Academy, Woolwich in 1910. He excelled at sport, including swimming, cricket, football, boxing and was a proficient horseman. Graduating from Woolwich he was commissioned into the Royal Engineers in August 1911. While attending the School of Military Engineering at Chatham he learned to fly at Hendon and in May 1914 was appointed to a course at CFS. He was rated as a very good pilot and above average as an officer. At the end of June 1914 he joined 5 Squadron and flew his machine to Amiens on 12 August when the RFC landed in France.

While at Woolwich and Chatham, one of Gordon's great friends was Lanoe Hawker (*Somme* page 81 and *Ypres* page 49), who was to earn the first Victoria Cross for aerial combat. It was during a dance at Woolwich that Lanoe met and fell for Bayly's sister Beatrice. On 4 August 1914 Gordon's father, who had been in failing health for some time, died and Lanoe went to the funeral. Just over two weeks later Mrs. Bayly suffered a second terrible blow when her son was reported missing in action. Lanoe obtained leave from CFS, where he was attending a course, and drove Beatrice and her mother to Mrs Bayly's sister.

In a letter to Beatrice on 22 September he wrote:

I am so glad if I have done any good, as my greatest pleasure is to do things that would earn Gordon's approval.

I am one with you in appreciating Gordon's splendid character. Never has anyone 'made good' like he did; never have I met such cheering optimism in face of any disappointment, an influence that will never depart from my life.

In April 1915 Lanoe, in an account of an attack on the well defended Zeppelin sheds at Gontrode in Belgium, finished with:

Gordon is still very much in my thoughts, and I am just beginning to be able to think of him without suffering agonies of grief, especially in my prayers when one naturally contemplates the beyond.

Lanoe Hawker would inevitably have married Beatrice but fate intervened when he was killed in action on 23 November 1916 by Manfred von Richthofen.

Waterfall and Bayly are assumed to have been brought down by German rifle fire from a body of troops who they were trying to reconnoitre.

Return to Junction 34 and onto the motorway towards Brussels on the E429-A8 until Junction 27, then right on the N7 to Bassilly. Continue on the N7 until there is a sign to the left to St Malcoult. Park here. The crash site is between the road and the ugly derelict industrial building.

La Croisette

On 2 September 1914, *The Aeroplane*, the popular British aeroplane weekly magazine, published this report:

The following letter appeared in the Morning Post of 1 September:

Sir, Last week in Belgium I saw a wrecked British aeroplane and beside it, the grave of the aviator. At the time I was prisoner with the Germans, and could not stop or ask questions. Later, with the object of establishing the identity of the aviator, I visited the place. Should after the war the family of the officer desire to remove his body, I am writing this that they may know where it is now buried.

The aeroplane fell close to the road between Enghien and Ath.

The report retrieved from the wreckage of Waterfall and Bayly's machine.

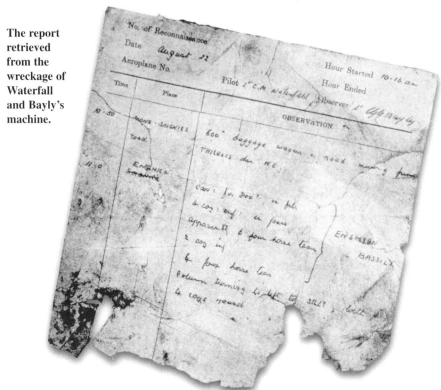

Waterfall and Bayly crashed next to this building. The original red brick tower has been incorporated into the derelict building.

Belgians near the place told me the officer was shot down by a column of German infantry, the strength of which column he was trying to discover. The aeroplane was totally destroyed, but on a twisted plate I found the words; 'Avro Manufacturing Company, Manchester, England'. There were also in the wreck paper forms for making out reports on reconnaissance. There was no writing on these, but the printed matter was in English.

At the head of the grave the Germans had put a wooden cross, on which they had written: 'Herr Flieger, 22nd August 1914'. The Belgians had covered the grave with flowers. It should not be difficult to find. It is on the left hand side of the road as one walks south from Enghien to Ath, in a pear orchard, near a very old red-brick house with a square tower. One hundred yards south of the graves is a signpost that reads, pointing south, 'Ath-14 kil.' Pointing north, 'Enghien-5 kil.' Enghien is about thirty kilometres south of Brussels. - Yours, & c.

RICHARD HARDING DAVIS
Correspondent 'New York Tribune'
10 Clarges Street, August 31st

The report written by Bayly was picked up near the crash by Belgians and forwarded to the War Office in London.

The Germans buried Waterfall and Bayly in a shallow grave but later the owner of the land where they were interred, exhumed their bodies and placed them in zinc-lined coffins. After the war the War Graves Commission removed them to Tournai, where they now fittingly lay side by side.

Return to the E429-A8 and continue towards Brussels. At Junction 26 go south on the N55 to Soignies, then the N6 to Mons. Join the E19-A7 at Junction 24 towards Paris and Tournai. Approaching Valenciennes leave at Junction 24 on the D101 to Onnaing, then left on the N30 to St Saulve and Valenciennes. Pass through St Saulve into Valenciennes and turn right at the traffic lights approximately 200 yards before a large church on the right side of the road. Go ahead at the next lights and follow signs to the cemetery.

Valenciennes (St. Roch) Communal Cemetery

The grave (II E5) we have come to visit concerns another of the large band of Americans who flew with the British and Commonwealth forces in the Great War.

From the civilian entrance take the right fork and go to the far end and the military cemetery. The casualty we have come to pay our respects to is two-thirds of the way down on the left side and is the fifth grave in from the hedge. Again the access to the cemetery is governed by the civilian burial ground opening hours and are approximately 0800 to 1645 hours, depending on the time of year.

Valenciennes was occupied by the Germans from the earliest days of the war until the Canadian Corps captured it at the beginning of November 1918. The 2nd, 57th, 4th Canadian and 32nd Casualty Clearing Stations were based here from November 1918 and the last of them did not leave until October 1919. The cemetery (17/8) contains 885 burials or commemorations from the First World War and a number of special memorials.

There is one particularly unusual white marble memorial on the shelter wall. At the outbreak of the Second World War the cemetery gardener was Robert Armstrong, an ex-Irish Guardsman, who held an Irish passport and, as Ireland was neutral, was allowed to continue with his work by the occupying German forces. However, his sympathies lay elsewhere and he helped Allied airmen and soldiers to escape, until arrested at the end of 1943. His death sentence was commuted to 15 years imprisonment and he was deported to Germany. He died in Waldheim Camp at the end of 1944. Armstrong was posthumously awarded the French *Medaille de Resistance Francaise*. The tablet was erected voluntarily by the people of the Valenciennes area.

Alvin Andrew Callender (II E5)

Callender is shown in Commonwealth War Graves records as being of United Kingdom nationality but in fact he was the son of Mr and Mrs James T Callender and was born in New Orleans on 4 July 1893 - an auspicious date, being United States Independence Day. After studying for a degree in architecture and being frustrated with the delays in joining up after the US declaration of war, he crossed the border into Canada and enlisted in the RFC. In June and July 1917 he completed his basic training on the campus of the University of Toronto. After flying training he was retained as an instructor and went with the Aerial Gunnery Squadron to Texas.

Agreement had been reached with the US government that, during the harsh Canadian winter, flying training would be transferred to the warmer

Alvin Callender with SE5a 'C' of 32 Squadron.

climate of the southern USA. In January 1918 Callender arrived in the United Kingdom and was posted to the Central Flying School at Upavon in Wiltshire. After further training he arrived at No. 32 Squadron based at Beauvois, northwest of Doullens, on 4 May 1918.

He settled in quickly and on 28 May claimed his first enemy machine, when he sent a Pfalz DIII down out of control. On 7 June he forced an enemy machine to land on the German side but shortly afterwards he was hit in the top wing fuel tank by an explosive bullet which set it on fire. Fortunately, the fire did not spread and eventually went out when the fuel was finished. Callender was able to return with enough petrol in his main tank. Five days later he was shot down, with eight bullet holes in the machine and one through the engine, causing it to fail. He returned to the squadron by car.

Despite the fact that it was summer, conditions in an open cockpit were gruelling, as he described in a letter to his sister:

> *Been cold too, lately. On the early patrol yesterday, escorting bombers, I felt my hands and feet were going to freeze off. One fellow, Brown, did get his face frozen, and today he won't come in the Mess, because he looks so funny we can't help laughing. His face from the forehead down is all black and blue and swollen up so he looks like a fat, black-face minstrel - However, it's nothing serious, and he gets a holiday until the swelling goes down.*

In another letter to his sister Callender illustrated the cosmopolitan nature of the RAF:

> *In the squadron now we have 6 Englishmen, 2 Scotchmen, 1 Irishman, 7 Canadians, 6 Americans, 2 Australians, and 1 South African. Pretty nearly every breed of white man there is, isn't it?*

Callender was on leave in the UK during the second half of August 1918 and on his return was promoted to command C Flight. On 27 September 32 Squadron escorted bombers during an attack on the aerodrome at Emerchicourt, during which they engaged the Fokker DVIIs of *Jasta* 5. Fritz Rumey, the unit's most successful pilot with 45 victories, got on Callender's tail but in doing so was shot up by Captain G E B Lawson. Rumey's aeroplane reared up and collided with the undercarriage of Lawson's machine, damaging his top wing. Rumey took to his parachute but this failed to deploy and he fell to his death (*Cambrai* page 79).

By the end of October Callender had claimed eight victories but on the

The pilots of *Jasta* Boelcke on 26 August 1918 shortly after the award of the *Pour le Mérite* to Karl Bolle the staffel commander. Second from left is Otto Löffler who claimed the DH9 from 49 Squadron. Seventh from the left is Karl Bolle. Eighth from the left is von Grieshiem, probable victor over Callender and on the extreme right is Alfred Lindenberger.

30th his luck ran out. Again 32 Squadron were escorting bombers, this time the DH9s of 49 Squadron. Fourteen machines took off, each carrying two 112 lb bombs to attack St Denis, near Mons. Their escort consisted of fourteen SE5as. Six of the DH9s turned back, mainly due to engine problems but the rest dropped their bombs on the target. Over Ghislain the formation was attacked by 30 Fokker biplanes and a furious dogfight took place. Three enemy machines were claimed by 32 Squadron and another shot down in flames by the DH9s. Unfortunately, one of the bombers went down in flames, with a wing falling off and the crew were killed. In addition three SE5s failed to return, with another pilot admitted to hospital as the result of wounds. Three SEs and a DH were claimed by pilots from *Jasta* Boelcke and it would seem that Callender probably fell victim to *Oberleutnant* von Griesheim.

The letters of Bogart Rogers, another American in the squadron, who had been in the patrol when Callender was killed, were published as *A Yankee Ace in the RAF*:

> *Thursday three of us went up to find Callender's grave and had very little trouble. His machine was crashed not far away, and we got mute testimony of what must have happened. It was badly crashed in a small field and it's probable the poor chap died in the air, or at least was unconscious. The machine had been simply shot to pieces, holes every where and some of them from explosive bullets. As far as we could see only one shot had hit him but as it must have entered his lungs it would have been enough. The grave was by a little farmhouse and not marked at all. We put up the cross and then sodded the top and built a little border of bricks around the*

edges. It was a solemn party that came home.

The cross was made from a four-bladed propeller and had attached to it a plate, made by the ground crew, recording Callender's details.

The loss of Callender was particularly sad in that he had completed nearly six months in France and was surely due to be returned to HE shortly. Also the end of the war was only twelve days away.

In 1978 Callender's letters were published in an excellent book entitled *War in an Open Cockpit*. See the 'Further Reading' section.

Retrace your steps along the N30 through St Saulve and turn right at the roundabout to the A2. Follow the motorway south to Paris. Leave at Junction 16.1 for Bouchain and follow signs onto the D943. Proceed through Bouchain and Aniche. Turn left at the roundabout in centre ville and continue on N45 to Lewarde. Turn left then immediate right on the D135 to Roucourt. Turn right at the cross roads, then turn left and stop at the entrance to the chateau.

Roucourt Aerodrome

Jagdstaffel 11 had been created on 28 September 1916 and became operational on 16 October in the 6 *Armee* sector. The first commanding

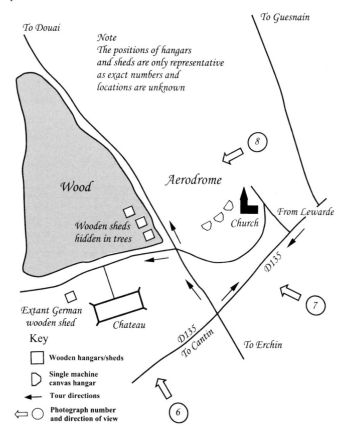

Picture No. 6: The chateau at Roucourt taken during the First World War, looking northwest.

Picture No. 7: Roucourt in 2003, looking northwest.

Picture No. 8: The machines of *Jasta* 12 at Roucourt with the hangars hidden in the trees behind.

officer was *Oberleutnant* Rudolf Emil Lang and its first base was Brayelle near Douai. On 15 January *Leutnant* Manfred von Richthofen took command. At this stage he was a rising star, having claimed sixteen victories with *Jasta* Boelcke and had been awarded the *Pour le Mérite* only two days before. Over the next few weeks he scored heavily and on 13 April 1917 claimed his 43rd victim, an FE2b of 25 Squadron. On this day the *staffel* moved to Roucourt, to the southeast of Douai, where they were to remain until 9 June.

This period was known to the RFC as Bloody April, because of their enormous casualties. They were employing obsolete aeroplanes against a well-equipped foe. The Battle of Arras had begun on 9 April and the high spot was the capture of Vimy Ridge by the Canadians. Richthofen claimed another ten victories while based at Roucourt but on 1 May he handed command of *Jasta* 11 to his brother Lothar and returned to Germany for well-deserved leave. While at home he was feted everywhere he went as a national hero.

While Manfred was away his unit continued to decimate Allied formations. Kurt Wolff shot down his 28th and 29th victims on 1 May and on 4 May received the *Pour le Mérite*. Lothar was severely wounded on 13

The burnt out shell of Roucourt after the war.

The German shed at Roucourt with Baron Becquet de Megille in the doorway. A window has been relocated from above the door and the doors themselves now slide instead of being hinged.

May and received his Blue Max the following day. Karl Allmenröder claimed fifteen victories in Manfred's absence and he received his Pour le Mérite on 4 June. During their sojourn at Roucourt *Jasta* 11 claimed about 80 Allied machines.

However, the British offensive shifted to the Flanders area, where they attacked at Messines on 7 June 1917. Consequently, *Jasta* 11 was moved to Harlebeke, near Courtrai, on 10 June to be closer to the action, which is where Manfred von Richthofen shortly rejoined them.

The family were evacuated from the chateau during the war and in 1918 it was burned out. The reason for this is unknown and the damage to the rear steps could be due to shell fire or bombing. The building was reduced to its stone foundations and rebuilt. The wing to one side was not renovated to its full height and some of the features visible in war time photographs no longer exist.

The father of the present owner, Baron Becquet de Megille, retrieved one of the sheds used by *Jasta* 11 in the adjacent wood and re-erected it on the farm to the west of the chateau. Though slightly modified, this is probably the only example of a First World War German air service building remaining and is a unique historical artefact.

I would remind visitors that the park, chateau and farm are private property and if you want to see the any of the buildings permission must be sought.

Continue ahead along the pave road. Cross the N43 to Goeulzin. At the T junction turn right then immediate left. At the next T junction go right then left again to Ferin. At the D956 left to Gouy s/s Bellonne. Continue on the D956 and at the D939 turn right for Arras. Vis-en-Artois Cemetery and Memorial will appear on the right.

Vis-en-Artois British Cemetery

The first grave we have come to visit (IX A26) is right at the far end of the cemetery and is the first one in Plot IX. When I was here in 2002 members of the present 32 Squadron RAF had placed a Poppy Appeal wooden cross on it.

Vis-en-Artois was taken by the Canadian Corps on 27 August 1918 and the cemetery (3/8) was begun immediately. The original 430 graves in Plots I and II comprise casualties from Canadian units and the Duke of Wellington's Regiment. After the armistice the cemetery was greatly enlarged with the bringing in of isolated battlefield burials, so that there are now 2,369 graves and commemorations of which 1,458 are unidentified.

The memorial at the rear of the cemetery commemorates over 9,000 British, Irish and South Africans lost from 8 August 1918 to the Armistice during the advance to victory in Picardy and Artois between Loos and the Somme who have no known grave.

Viscount Glentworth (IX A26)

Edmond William Claude Gerard de Vere was the eldest son of the 4th Earl of Limerick and was born on 14 October 1894. He served as an observer with 14 Squadron RFC in Palestine from 31 May until 5 October 1916, having spent some time on loan to No. 1 Squadron Australian Flying Corps. On returning to the UK he attended the School of Military Aeronautics at Reading and on 10 June 1917 was sent to Vendome in France for flying training. After advanced training he was posted to 32 Squadron in France on 13 October 1917, flying the De Havilland DH5 with its distinctive back-staggered upper wing. For reasons unknown he was only with the squadron for two months before posting back to the UK on 17 December. He was then posted to 7 Training Depot Squadron as an

The pilots of 32 Squadron. Glentworth is fourth from the left, G E B Lawson eleventh from the left and Bogart Rogers thirteenth from the left.

assistant instructor, and then rejoined 32 Squadron on 22 February 1918. By this time the DH5 had been replaced by the much superior Royal Aircraft Factory SE5a.

On 1 April 1918, the day the Royal Air Force was created, Glentworth was flying on a patrol when he observed four enemy scouts attacking two SE5s. He immediately dived on one which went down to 50 feet off the ground and then flattened out. Glentworth kept on the enemy's tail and fired 50 rounds at very close range, following which it crashed into a wood.

Glentworth's last flight occurred on 18 May. It was a morning offensive patrol taking off at 0830 hours from Beauvois, and consisted of twelve SE5s. One of the pilots was Bogart Rogers whom we met on page 61 when he was in the fight during which Alvin Callender was killed. Another member of this fateful patrol was Captain G E B Lawson (see page 60). There were a number of indecisive engagements with enemy scouts and two-seaters. Lieutenant P Hooper and Glentworth attacked two enemy two-seaters over Etaing, with Hooper firing 60 rounds into one at very close range. It made off in an easterly direction. Hooper saw pieces coming off Glentworth's aircraft, which then went down in a spin and was last seen at 10,000 feet still spinning. Three SE5s failed to return from the patrol but it was discovered that Lawson had had his engine knocked out by enemy gunfire though he was able to reach Allied lines, where he crashed without injury. Another pilot became lost and landed at another aerodrome to refuel, returning later that afternoon. Unfortunately, Glentworth failed to return.

In 1996 Bogart Rogers' letters were published as *A Yankee Ace in the RAF*. On 2 December 1918 he wrote:

> *Yesterday the C.O. and I went up into the awful area to look for the grave of Viscount Glentworth who was shot down just after I came to the squadron in May. We found it and what was left of the machine and put up a cross. He was the son of Earl and Lady Limerick and a fine chap. The country is pretty awful, and there were still a couple of Huns that had been overlooked.*

Bernard Joseph Tolhurst (XI E7)

The next grave we have come to see is in the extension at the far left of the cemetery and is connected with a disastrous day in the history of No.11 Squadron RFC.

The air campaign for the Battle of Arras began on 4 April 1917. The RFC had concentrated their resources and were numerically superior to the opposing German forces. Unfortunately, much of the British equipment was obsolescent. Better machines in the shape of the SE5, Bristol Fighter and the DH5 were held back until the commencement of the offensive.

With the constant offensive policy, RFC losses were very heavy and the month became known as Bloody April. Of the 319 aircrew lost in this period, 252 were killed on the German side of the lines or taken prisoner.

No. 11 Squadron, based at Le Hameau (see page 140), were involved in reconnaissance and photography. By the 22 April they had lost three crews, with another three members wounded, plus one killed, but on this day suffered terrible losses with seven men wounded, one died of wounds and one crew missing in action. They made three attempts to reconnoitre the Drocourt - Queant line and one must question the wisdom of repeatedly sending machines to the same target. The missing FE2b was flown by Sergeant John Kenneth Hollis and his observer Lieutenant Bernard Joseph Tolhurst. The squadron had the misfortune to encounter the highly experienced and proficient *Jasta* 11, based at Roucourt (see the previous

B J Tolhurst

entry in the chapter), led by Manfred von Richthofen. Von Richthofen sent one FE down to crash just on the British side of the lines with a wounded crew and Kurt Wolff brought down Hollis and Tolhurst. It was his nineteenth victory and on 4 May he received the *Pour le Mérite.*

Bernard Tolhurst, born on 17 March 1891, was educated at Stonyhurst and was a keen sportsman, especially of cricket. At Exeter College, Oxford, he played cricket, football and hockey for the college. Shortly after the outbreak of war he was commissioned into the 11th Battalion Duke of Wellington's Regiment and served with them during the Battle of the Somme. In early 1917 Tolhurst transferred to the RFC and after training at Reading and Hythe was posted to France on 5 April. He was to last just over two weeks.

FE2 No. 4993 of 11 Squadron at Le Hameau, with Lieutenant B A Taylor and his observer Corporal Ross.

John Hollis had served nearly two years in France with 16 Squadron RFC. Following flying training he was posted to France, barely one month after graduating and with only 40 hours flying experience. He survived a month before becoming a casualty.

In July 1918 Hollis wrote to Tolhurst's father from Soltau, near Hanover:

This letter may come as something of a surprise to you. I ought to have written to you before but for several months after my capture I was too ill to do anything, and have only just managed to get your address from the Record Office through the R.F.C. Prisoners Committee.

I will endeavour to the best of my ability to give you a few details regarding the death of your son, Lt. B. J. Tolhurst, who was with me as Observer when I was brought down on 22nd. April 1917.

I must first let you know that I did not know your son's name until I received it from Records a couple of days ago, as I was rather badly wounded in the head and have been suffering from partial loss of memory since so you will understand that I

Corporal, later Sergeant J K Hollis.

am trusting entirely to my information from records and I sincerely hope that this letter will comfort you to a certain extent.

We (your son and I) left the Aerodrome on Sunday afternoon at 3 p.m. with six other machines to do a photographic reconnaissance in the Arras district.

At about 3.45 p.m. we commenced an action with a squadron of German aeroplanes far in excess of our own number. Your son was one of the first to open fire, from my machine: after a few minutes fighting the enemy with a great burst of fire cut my two chief controls, thereby rendering my machine somewhat uncontrollable.

I myself stopped a bullet in the shoulder, but we continued fighting, your son keeping wonderfully cool. A little later he (your son) was hit, and my engine almost stopped. By this time we were practically at the enemy's mercy, as the engine had been hit, and I had only one remaining control, which was cut a little later. Your son, however, who had control of our machine guns, was still fighting well, despite the fact he was badly wounded, and weak from loss of blood.

The firing still went on as heavily as ever, but I thought we might just manage to reach our lines, as we were gliding in the right direction. Your son was too weak to stand, but he continued using one of his guns while on his knees and did some very effective work.

As we neared the ground I saw that we should not reach our lines, and tried to tell Mr Tolhurst but found he was unconscious. I tried to throw the guns over the side but was unable to stand as I had received 4 wounds altogether.

Shortly afterwards we struck the ground, being less than 1/2 a mile on the wrong side. We were both thrown out, and I got a crack on the head which knocked me silly. How long I remained so I cannot tell.

When I recovered, however, Mr Tolhurst was lying a few yards away from me. We were between two of the enemy's trenches.

We were taken by the (Germans) into the nearest trench.

While we were there, your son (who had not been hurt by the fall) recovered consciousness, and asked me how I felt. I answered that " I felt shot all over" and he said "So do I" He asked for a drink and I gave him a flask of spirits that I always carried. We were later taken into a dug out and received medical attention. When the doctor had finished me, I was carried into an adjoining room. The German doctor very shortly came to see me and he said Mr Tolhurst these words "Your friend I am afraid is going to die: he has been shot 3 times in the stomach" He was soon brought in and laid beside me on a stretcher, but was unconscious and a little delirious. He never recovered again and died muttering "Got one, Got one".

I shall ever regret Mr Tolhurst not having obtained some small article of clothing or equipment from him to send to you but believe me I was in great pain myself and very dazed.

Your son Mr Tolhurst, died like a hero, and it was really a marvellous piece of work his fighting so well and so long when he was so badly wounded.

I hope when I return to England to see you so that I may give you fuller details.

I am afraid that this letter will sound very crude and unsatisfactory but I hope that the knowledge that your son died like a hero will be of some solace to you.

Believe me I sympathise deeply with you and regret that the necessity should have arisen to give you these painful details.

On 17 August 1918, Tolhurst's father wrote to the War Office advising them that they had received a letter from Hollis, and in it said:

It's a very interesting letter and though very sad for his parents yet we feel very proud that our boy died so bravely.

After his release from prisoner of war camp, Hollis wrote a much fuller account of his last flight in a letter to Tolhurst's father on 20 February 1919, and concluded:

Game to the last, fighting on his knees when he could no longer

The
telegram
that every
family who
had a loved
one fighting
in the war
dreaded.

A telegram form (O.H.M.S. POST OFFICE TELEGRAPHS) reading: "TO Tolhurst. Ditton Court Farm Ditton near Maidstone. Regret to inform you Lt B J Tolhurst West Riding Regt Regt att R.F.C. 11 Sqd missing April twenty-second aaa This does not necessarily mean either killed or wounded aaa any further news sent when received. FROM Secretary, War Office."

stand, and even when he was dying he thought of duty, and must have been consoled in the knowledge that he had done his duty as few could have done.

I hope in the afterworld to meet him so that I may tell him how I appreciate wonderful pluck and devotion to duty, and how through his wonderful staying and fighting powers he saved my own life.

Continue ahead on the D939 and turn right on the D33 to Monchy-le-Preux. Follow the D33 to Roeux and in the village turn left by the green War Graves Commission signs. Proceed over motorway and under railway and Brown's Copse will appear on the right.

Brown's Copse Cemetery

The special memorial we have come to visit is half way down the right hand side of the cemetery (2/67) against the wall and is the second from the right in a row of eight. It commemorates H D Harvey-Kelly, the first RFC pilot to land in France. The stone is marked *Known To Be Buried In This Cemetery*, as the exact location of his grave has been lost. On my last visit the headstone was very worn and the inscription barely readable.

The cemetery is named after a small copse (the Bois Rossignol) on the eastern side and contains 2,068 burials or commemorations, of which 858 are unknown.

Hubert Dunsterville Harvey-Kelly

In *Airfields and Airmen, Somme* page 109, there is an account of how Harvey-Kelly secured the honour of being the first RFC pilot in France, by

71

Harvey-Kelly (left).

cutting across country and thus incurring the wrath of his squadron commander, Major C J Burke. The reader should see the next section in this book for a biography of Burke.

Harvey-Kelly was born on 9 February 1891. Commissioned into the Royal Irish Regiment in October 1910, he transferred to the reserve of the RFC in 1913. He gained his Royal Aero Club 'ticket', No.501, on 30 May the same year. On his return from France Harvey-Kelly became an instructor with No. 4 Reserve Aeroplane Squadron, then 18 Squadron and finally 14 Squadron at Gosport

He then returned to France as a flight commander with 3 Squadron, who were operating Moranes of various types.

In his autobiography *Flying and Soldiering* R R Money had this to say of him:

Morane squadrons specialised in Flight-Commanders who were full of character: Harvey-Kelly was one: he had a custom of spitting over the side of his machine if a burst of Archie came very near, and one day he returned because, he said, he had no spit left. He went on leave from France on one occasion, and was told to report to London Headquarters at the expiration of his leave. He did not turn up, so a kindly Staff sent him orders by post. He did not acknowledge these, nor did he report for duty; so the kind Staff, rather worried, sent someone else in his place and posted fresh orders to Harvey-Kelly. For three weeks they tried to find him, and telegrams and orders were waiting for him in every well-known hotel and bar in London. Eventually he turned up at the War Office one day in a highly aggrieved state, and flung a handful of contradictory telegrams and letters on the table asking how in the name of O'Brien Og could he go to all of those places at once, and anyway, he was fed up with England and wanted to go back to the War. They let him.

He lived to command a Squadron and to be killed in the air, and I have always been of the opinion that he was one of the "mad Majors" whose doings became almost mythical among the infantry.

Harvey-Kelly returned to the UK and spent some time with 1 Reserve Squadron, followed by command of 56 Squadron. On 31 January 1917 he left this unit on appointment as commanding officer of 19 Squadron. They had been operating the RAF BE12, and suffered heavy casualties but re-equipped in October 1916 with the French Spad. (*Cambrai*, page 152.)

The Spad 7

The first Spad type 7 flew in April 1916 and it was powered by the new, superb 150hp Hispano-Suiza engine. It was fitted with a single Vickers machine gun synchronised to fire through the propeller. The RFC were quick to realise the potential of the design and within days asked for three examples of it. The first machine was delivered on 9 September 1916 and flew with 60 Squadron for a month before being sent to England. Further examples followed, but delivery was slow due to the French having to supply their own units as well and 19 Squadron were not fully equipped until February 1917, when Harvey-Kelly arrived. The only other RFC squadron to have a full complement of Spads was No. 23, who received all theirs by April 1917. Such was the need for fighter machines, contracts were placed by both the RFC and RNAS with British firms to manufacture the Spad under licence. Some British-built samples reached RFC squadrons in France but had a poorer performance than the French examples and were nose heavy. They were not greatly liked and a decision was made to supply only French-built aeroplanes.

Spad eventually produced the type 13, which employed the 200hp geared Hispano Suiza 8b and had two Vickers machine guns. It had a much better performance and was also quickly ordered by the RFC. Unfortunately, deliveries were again slow and only one RFC unit, No. 23, was fully equipped with the type. In November 1917, 19 Squadron converted to the Sopwith Dolphin, followed by 23 Squadron in April 1918.

In RFC service the Spad did not seem to have been the success it was with the French and Americans. For more details of the Spad type 13 see *Airfields and Airmen, The Channel Coast,* Chapter Two, La Lovie Aerodrome.

A Black Day for 19 Squadron

Harvey-Kelly arrived at 19 Squadron on 2 February 1917. They were based at Vert Galand (*Somme*, page 45) and formed part of 9 (Headquarters) Wing. This was moved around the front to bolster the RFC

Spad A6633 of 19 Squadron showing the unit marking of a black dumbbell. On 19 March 1917 this became the first RFC Spad lost to enemy action when Second Lieutenant S S B Purves was taken prisoner.

in a given area, in much the same way von Richthofen's *Jagdgeschwader* 1 was employed.

The Spad initially suffered gun problems, with jams being a frequent occurrence. Their first success was gained on 24 March, when Lieutenant A H Orlebar claimed a probable victory when he attacked a single-seater near Douai. The first combat loss had happened five days earlier when Second Lieutenant S S B Purves failed to return from a patrol and was later found to have been taken prisoner. While the RFC was incurring horrendous casualties in Bloody April 19 Squadron had escaped lightly, losing only one machine to enemy action. However, on 29 April they suffered a heavy blow.

Squadron commanders were technically not allowed to fly on operations, though many did. Harvey-Kelly was one of these and in the morning of 29 April he took off on patrol with two other pilots. They had the bad luck to meet von Richthofen and his *jasta*. All three Spads were brought down, with Harvey-Kelly and Richard Applin being killed, and William Norman Hamilton being taken prisoner. Applin has no known grave and his name appears on the Air Services Memorial to the Missing at Arras. After he returned from captivity Hamilton recounted what had happened:

> *OP between Douai and Cambrai. Major Harvey-Kelly leading, sighted and attacked Richthofen's circus 14-strong over Epinoy. Lieutenant Applin was shot down at once and killed. Circus split up, half on the Major, half on me. My guns gave repeated No. 4's, eventually a No. 2; I had shot down one HA but then gun jammed hopelessly over Douai, so made for the line, having lost the Major who was shot down and died three days later in a German hospital. Both my tanks were holed and I had to land.*

Harvey-Kelly fell victim to Kurt Wolff as his 24th victory. Some of his other victims who appear in the *Airfields and Airmen* series are D M Tidmarsh of 48 Squadron (*Somme*, page 78), French and Harding of 25 Squadron (*Somme*, page 63), together with Hollis and Tolhurst in the Vis-en-Artois entry earlier in this chapter.

Kurt Wolff

Wolff was born on 6 February 1895 and in March 1912 became a cadet in *Eisenbahm* Regiment Nr. 4. In April 1915 he was commissioned and during July transferred to the air service. He survived a crash in which his instructor was killed. After service in a two-seater unit on the Verdun front, Wolff was posted to *Jasta* 11 on 5 November 1916. Prior to Manfred von Richthofen taking command he failed to claim any victories but, following the first success, scored at an amazing rate. Between 6 March and 1 May he shot down 29 machines, of which 22 were in Bloody April. Wolff was

Wolff in his Fokker Triplane, though all his claims were made while flying the Albatros scout.

awarded the Knight's Cross with Swords of the Royal Hohenzollern House Order on 26 April and the *Pour le Mérite* on 4 May. Promotion to command of *Jasta* 29 followed, but he returned to *Jasta* 11, as commanding officer, on 2 July. Wounded on 11 July in the left hand by a Triplane of 10 Naval, Wolff returned two months later, but failed to add to his total of 33 victories. His meteoric career came to an end on 15 September 1917 in action with machines from 70 Squadron RFC and 10 Naval. Flight Sub Lieutenant N M MacGregor of 10 Naval shot him down near Wervicq, southeast of Ypres. Wolff was MacGregor's first claim in 10 Naval, though he had shot down four enemy machines while with 6 Naval. He survived the war having been awarded a Distinguished Service Cross.

Wolff's Triplane was the first of the type to be lost in combat. His body was taken back to Germany for burial.

Continue through Fampoux and turn left on the D42 to Athies and then through St-Laurent-Blangy. At the roundabout turn right on the D60 for Bailleul-Sir-Berthoult. Pass under the motorway on the D919 to Roclincourt. Turn right at Bailleul Road Cemetery to the German cemetery.

Leutnant **Kurt Wolff in his room at Roucourt. The two numbers on the wall, A3338, were removed from the Bristol F2a of D M Tidmarsh, who was taken prisoner on 11 April 1917 (*Somme*, page 78).**

St-Laurent-Blangy German Cemetery

This is another very large cemetery with a total of 31,939 burials and is divided by the *Kameradengräb* or mass grave, containing 24,870 bodies, of which half are unknown. There are six plots numbered from I to VI, with three across the front and the other three behind. The area beyond the *Kameradengräb* is raised and the grave we have come to visit (VI/33) is in the far right corner.

Kurt Schönfelder *Jasta* 7 (VI/33)

In the early days of single-seater German aeroplanes and then the *KEKs* there were a number of German naval pilots flying with the German army air service. One of these was Kurt Schönfelder. On his headstone his rank is shown as *flieger*, though in fact he was an *Oberflügmeister*, a naval rank.

Born on 30 July 1894 at Toschen he had learned to fly in December 1913, gaining licence No. 634. He joined *Jasta* 7 in August 1916 and was to remain with them until he was killed on 26 June 1918.

Jasta 7 was created on 26 August 1916 and was mobilised the following month. Its first victory was scored on 23 October. On 21 July 1917 the first commanding officer, *Oberleutnant* Fritz von Bronsart-Schellendorf, was killed and *Leutnant* Josef Jacobs, who had claimed four victories with *Jasta* 22, was appointed to command. He was to remain in charge for the rest of the war. Of the total of approximately 120 victories credited to the *staffel*, Jacobs was to claim a third, and in the process earned the *Pour le Mérite*.

Schönfelder's first three claims, in March and May 1917, were unconfirmed. His first official victory was on 22 July, when he shot down an SE5a of 56 Squadron. The pilot, Second Lieutenant R G Jardine, was killed and has no known grave, his name appearing on the Air Forces Memorial to the Missing at Arras. By June 1918 Schönfelder was credited with thirteen victories, the last being a Sopwith

Kurt Schönfelder, *Jasta* 7.

Camel of 210 Squadron, the pilot of which was taken prisoner.

By chance, five days later, on 26 June, *Jasta* 7 encountered 210 Squadron again and this time Schönfelder was the victim. Fifteen Camels took off from their aerodrome at Ste-Marie-Cappel (See *Airfields and Airmen: The Channel Coast*, Chapter Three) for an evening offensive patrol and encountered a formation of Fokker biplanes. A combat report described the action:

> *Patrol attacked 6 E.A. over Armentieres at 12,000 ft. at 7.20 p.m.*
>
> *Capt. Coombes and Lieuts. Sanderson and Unger got on the tail of one of them and together fired about 300 rounds into him. E.A. went down in a slow spin, then in a series of stalls and dives, and finally crashed about 1 mile W. of Armentieres.*

The credit was shared between the three Camel pilots. The German view of the action was described in Jacob's diary:

> *Our entire Jagdstaffel grieves today because of the loss of Obflm. Schönfelder in combat.*
>
> *We had taken off for a sortie, and, in the vicinity of Ypres, a squadron of 15 to 20 Englishmen were sighted dropping bombs on our side of the lines. We manoeuvred for position, gaining some altitude, but were immediately jumped by 3 Sopwith Camels. I blazed away at one of the Camels who was slowly spiralling down when I saw a Fokker D-VII drop by me with his right top wing disintegrating. I recognised the aircraft as one belonging to Obflm. Schönfelder by the beautiful golden star on the black fuselage of the Fokker. Seeing that Schönfelder's aircraft was totally disabled, I had to resume combat with my adversary who was now in a steep dive toward Menin. As he attempted to straighten out, several times, I jabbed away with both guns until the wings of the Camel folded up*

and the wreckage crashed into the ground at the Castle Park in Menin. When I later visited the wreckage, there were only a few fragments, and, next to it, lay the dead body of Lt. Brothman (sic) who was 19 years old and belonged to 210 Squadron R.A.F. He had fought very courageously, this Camel was my 22nd victory.

Upon arriving back at the base, I learned that Schönfelder had fallen near Bousbecque and that his machine, a complete wreck, had hit a house.

Clarence Duckworth Boothman is buried in Pont-du-Hem Military Cemetery, grave number IV H31 (*Ypres*, page 102).

Jacobs survived the war and died on 29 July 1978.

Lieutenant Kenneth Russell Unger

Kenneth Unger.

Unger was an American, from Newark, New Jersey and was born on 19 April 1898. Despite the fact he held US Aero Club certificate No. 1356, he was turned down by the US military. Like many other Americans he crossed into Canada and enlisted in the RFC. After training in Canada and Texas he arrived at 210 Squadron on 8 June 1918. The first of his claims was Schönfelder's Fokker biplane and he claimed another three on the same day. The pilots in this patrol were involved in another incident on 23 July 1918 (see *Airfields and Airmen, The Channel Coast*, Chapter Two, Ramskapelle Road Military Cemetery) when the noted 210 Squadron ace, H T Mellings, was killed. Unger spent a short time in hospital during August and then on 14 October fired 100 rounds into a black Fokker Triplane. Though claimed as an out of control, this was almost certainly Josef Jacobs again, who escaped unscathed. By the Armistice Unger had fourteen victories to his credit and been awarded the British DFC. Between the wars he flew the US Air Mail and during the Second World War piloted transport aeroplanes for the US Navy, with the rank of lieutenant commander. He died on 6 January 1979 in Florida.

For a full biography of Unger I recommend *Madison Ace* by Michael O'Neill in *Over the Front*, volume 14, page 196.

Laurence Percival Coombes

L P Coombes. He is wearing the early form of DFC ribbon with horizontal stripes.

Born on 9 April 1899 in India, he was educated at the City of London School. He joined the RNAS on 2 July 1917 and after training at Crystal Palace, Chingford and Cranwell joined 12 Naval. Shortly afterwards he was posted to 10 Naval and scored one victory with this unit before it became 210 Squadron upon the formation of the RAF on 1 April 1918. On 31 July he claimed a last victory, his fifteenth, having been promoted to flight commander and received a DFC. He spent the remainder of the war with 204 Training Depot Station and was demobilised on 17 April 1919. Attending London University he completed an engineering degree and joined the Royal Aircraft Establishment. In 1938 he was asked by the Australian government to establish an aeronautical research laboratory and became Chief Supervisor at the Aero Research Laboratory. He died in Melbourne on 2 June 1988.

Ivan Couper Sanderson

Born on 21 December 1899, Sanderson came from Gerrard's Cross in Buckinghamshire. He joined the RNAS at Greenwich on 24 October 1917, aged only seventeen. Part of his flying tuition was conducted at the RNAS flying training school at Vendome in France. He crossed to France at the end of April 1918 and joined 210 Squadron on 9 May. Claiming eleven victories by early September, he was wounded on the 17th of that month and admitted to the Queen Alexandra Hospital at Dunkirk. Invalided to the UK on 28 September, he was demobilised in April 1919. He died on 25 January 1968.

Retrace your steps under the motorway and turn left on the N39 to Douai. The cemetery will appear behind a concrete crash barrier on the right. Continue for 100 yards past it and pull into a parking area on the right.

Point-du-Jour Military Cemetery

The grave we are visiting (III C2) is in the far right corner of the cemetery (2/61), adjacent to the seat. This grave dates from the earliest days of the RFC and its predecessors.

The area was captured during the Battle of Arras in April 1917 and remained in Allied hands until the end of the war. Point-du-Jour was a house on the Gavrelle to St-Laurent-Blangy road. Two cemeteries were established here and were in use from April to November 1917 and again in May 1918. At the armistice it contained 82 graves which now form Plot I. As with many other cemeteries it was enlarged with battlefield graves and from other small burial grounds and now contains 763 First World War graves or commemorations, of which 372 are unknowns.

On 21 March 2002, twenty-three unknown soldiers were buried here after their remains were found by French archaeologists and they complete rows 4C, 4D and 4E.

Charles John Burke (III C2)

Burke was born on 9 March 1882. After service in the militia he obtained a commission in the Royal Irish Regiment on 26 September 1903. Promotion to lieutenant followed on 15 June 1904 and to captain on 22 December 1909. From July 1905 until December 1909 he served with the West African Frontier Force. He was employed at the Aeroplane and Balloon School from November 1910 until March 1911 and then joined the Air Battalion of the Royal Engineers, having gained his French flying certificate, No.260, on 4 October 1910. With the formation of the Royal Flying Corps on 12 May 1912, he became a founder member.

By the outbreak of war in August 1914 he was a very experienced aviator and as senior RFC squadron commander led them to France. However, as we have seen in the previous entry, he was thwarted by Harvey-Kelly in his ambition to be the first RFC pilot to land in France.

With the reorganisation of the RFC structure, Burke became commanding officer of 2 Wing on 9 November 1914 with the rank of lieutenant-colonel. On 1 February 1915 he was awarded a Distinguished Service Order, having already been twice Mentioned in Despatches. At the beginning of February 1916 he was given the vital job of commandant of the Central Flying School. Promotion to Brigadier-General and command of an RFC brigade in France must surely have been imminent.

Unfortunately, casualties in the BEF had been so great that there was a crying need for experienced officers and Burke returned to the army in command of 1/ East Lancashire Regiment,

On 9 April 1917, during the Battle of Arras, the battalion moved up in support, consolidating the area taken since the initial assault. During the

The aviation pioneers of 2 Squadron, Montrose, May 1914. Several of them appear in the *Airfields and Airmen* series. At the rear left is H D Harvey-Kelly (see page 71 and *Somme*, pages 56 and 108.) Third from the right at the rear is M W Noel (*Cambrai*, page 46). In the centre, front row is C J Burke, the commanding officer. On his left is Ferdie Waldron (*Cambrai*, page 167.) Burke was known in the RFC as 'Pregnant Percy'.

night of 8/9 April there had been no enemy shelling but in the morning a number of accurate rounds fell on B Company digging in near the remains of the Point-du-Jour house. The company commander was killed and at 1645 hours a burst practically wiped out No. 6 Platoon. Shortly after, another shell killed the battalion commander and his orderly, Lance Corporal R Pentland, together with a lot of men from the right, front post of B Company, which Burke was visiting. Total casualties amounted to two officers killed and two wounded, plus about 55 other ranks killed and wounded. Pentland, a Canadian from Toronto, lies in the grave next to Burke.

With the benefit of hindsight, it would have been better to employ Burke's experience as a senior RFC officer within the rapidly expanding flying corps, rather than with an infantry battalion.

This completes the tour. Return to Arras on the N39. A visit to the 9th Scottish memorial, 300 metres to the east, provides a short cut back onto the opposite carriageway for Arras.

The Northern Area

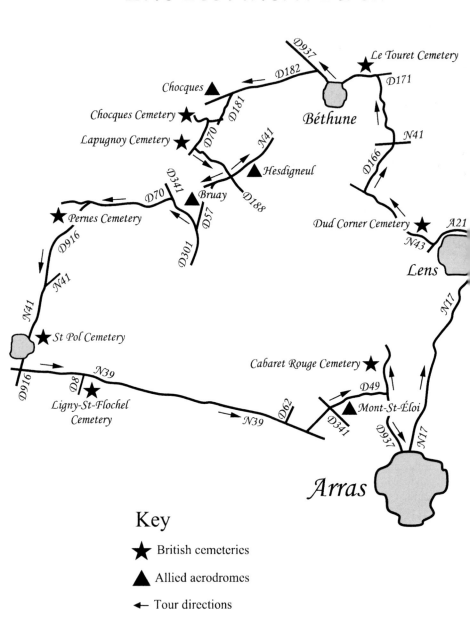

Chocques

Chocques Cemetery

Lapugnoy Cemetery

D937

D182

D181

D70

D341

D70

Pernes Cemetery

D916

N41

N41

St Pol Cemetery

D916

D8

N39

Ligny-St-Flochel
Cemetery

N39

D62

N41

Hesdigneul

Bruay

D188

D57

D301

Le Touret Cemetery

D171

Béthune

N41

D166

Dud Corner Cemetery

N43

A21

Lens

N17

Cabaret Rouge Cemetery

D49

Mont-St-Éloi

D341

D937

N17

Arras

Key

★ British cemeteries

▲ Allied aerodromes

← Tour directions

Chapter Two

ARRAS: NORTHERN AREA

This itinerary covers the part of the front that remained firmly in Allied hands for the whole war. The route passes through the heavily industrialised area around Lens and Bethune with its familiar slag heaps. On this tour the places that will be visited and the main points of interest are:

Dud Corner Cemetery - A M Read VC
Le Touret Military Cemetery - B H Barrington-Kennett
Chocques Aerodrome - 3 Squadron and the Portuguese Flying Corps
Chocques Military Cemetery - A bomb accident
Lapugnoy Military Cemetery - Brigadier-General G S Shephard
Hesdigneul Aerodrome - A A McLeod VC and King George V
Bruay Aerodrome - 40 Squadron
Pernes British Cemetery - R S Dallas, naval ace
St Pol Communal Cemetery Extension - Hughes and Sandy, 69 Squadron
Ligny-St-Flochel British Cemetery - L P Watkins and the Zeppelin L48
Mont-St-Éloi Aerodrome - 8 Naval Squadron
Cabaret Rouge British Cemetery - Kennedy and Tilney, 40 Squadron RFC

Leave Arras on the N17 towards Lens. The N17 becomes the A21 to Calais. Exit at Junction 8 on the N43 towards Bethune. Continue ahead and Dud Corner is on the right.

Dud Corner Cemetery

The grave we are visiting (VII F19) is six rows from the front and is the second grave from the centre aisle. It contains the remains of one of the August 1914 RFC pioneers. The name of the cemetery (2/7) is believed to refer to the large number of unexploded German shells found here after the Armistice.

The walls of the cemetery form the Loos Memorial and commemorate the 20,000 officers and men who have no known grave and were lost in the area from the Lys River and the old southern boundary of the First Army, east and west of Grenay.

There were only five burials during the war but, as with most cemeteries, it was greatly expanded with isolated battlefield casualties and other small burial grounds, until now there are nearly 2,000 casualties commemorated here.

Anketell Moutray Read VC (VII F19)

Read was born on 27 October 1884 at Bampton, Devon and was the son of a colonel. Entering Sandhurst in 1901, he was gazetted into the Gloucester Regiment in late 1903. He was a boxer of distinction and, while stationed in India, won the championship eight times at heavyweight and twice at middleweight, winning at both weights in the same meetings. When back in the UK, he won the Army and Navy Heavyweight Championship three times. In 1912 he took flying lessons on a Bristol Biplane at the Bristol School, Brooklands, gaining his Royal Aero Club certificate, No. 336, on 22 October. After the outbreak of war he went to France with No. 3 Squadron. During the fighting on the Aisne in September 1914 he was severely wounded while attached to the 9th Lancers.

A M Read VC.

During April 1915 he returned to his old unit, 1/Northants Regiment, probably for the same reason as C J Burke in the previous chapter, that there was a desperate shortage of experienced officers, due to heavy casualties.

P E Butcher who went to France with 2 Squadron as an air mechanic at the beginning of the war, had this to say of Read in his autobiography, *Skill and Devotion*:

> *Our new equipment, which arrived before September, gave us a mixed collection of B.E.2A's, 2Bs and 2Cs, numbering six machines each to our three Flights, which were all part of a big new build-up for a fresh offensive, that was to become known as the Battle of Loos. Before it opened on September 25th, we had a pleasant surprise in a visit from our former O.C., Training, Captain A.M. Reid. (sic)*
>
> *This was the officer who had, while recovering from a crash, been in charge of our early instruction at home and had marched with us when we took, from Gun Hill to Aldershot for burial, the two officers whom I had seen collide and fall on to the golf course before the war.*
>
> *Now, the Captain was no longer with us, having gone back to his old regiment, the Northamptons. Before going into action he was pleased to shake each of us old boys by the hand, wishing us the very best of luck. Alas, we were never to see him again, as the V.C. we were proud to afterwards hear he had won, was a posthumous award.*

The title of Butcher's book was taken from a letter A M Read had written to him.

On 25 September 1/ Northants attacked enemy trenches north of Loos, after the initial assaulting battalions had made little headway, due to the presence of gas. The German wire was intact and impossible to get through, so the Northants were forced to lie down in open ground for some hours, suffering considerable casualties in the process. It was during this period that Read earned his Victoria Cross. The citation, gazetted on 15 November 1915, read:

> *For most conspicuous bravery during the first attack near Hulluch on the morning of 25th September, 1915. Although partially gassed, Captain Read went out several times in order to rally parties of different units which were disorganised and retiring. He led them back into the firing line, and utterly regardless of danger, moved freely about encouraging them under a withering fire. He was mortally wounded while carrying out this gallant work. Captain Read had previously shown conspicuous bravery during digging operations on 29th, 30th and 31st August, 1915, and on the night of the 29th-30th July he carried out of action an officer, who was mortally wounded, under a hot fire from rifles and grenades.*

It is believed that he was killed by a sniper.

Continue ahead on the N43 to Noyelles-les-Vermelles and turn right to Annequin on the D166. Turn right on the N41 and then left on the D166 to Cuinchy. Proceed ahead through Cuinchy and Festubert, then turn left on the D171 to Le Touret, which is on the right.

Le Touret Military Cemetery

The grave we are visiting here (II D13) is that of another pioneer airman who returned to his old regiment and fell in action. It is situated in the right hand corner of the cemetery, in the middle of a row abeam the Cross of Sacrifice.

The cemetery (15/40) was started in November 1914 by the Indian Corps and was in continuous use until March 1918, when the area fell into German hands. Further burials were made in late 1918. The cemetery originally contained 264 Portuguese graves which were moved to their National Cemetery at Richebourg-L'Avoue. There are a total of over 900 First World War casualties commemorated here.

The Le Touret Memorial is located on the left side of the cemetery and records the names of over 13,000 men who fell in this area before 25 September 1915, who have no known grave. This number does not include the Canadian and Indian unknowns who are commemorated on their own memorials at Vimy Ridge and Neuve-Chapelle. On Panel 17 is recorded the name of Second Lieutenant F H Lawrence, who was killed on 9 May 1915 and was the brother of T E Lawrence (*Cambrai*, page 66).

Basil Herbert Barrington-Kennett (II D13)

Barrington-Kennett was born on 9 November 1884 in Brighton. He attended Eton from September 1899 until April 1902 and in 1907 was gazetted into the Grenadier Guards. He was another pre-war flier, having taken his 'ticket' on a Bleriot Monoplane at Hendon on 31 December 1910, his licence being No.43. 'B-K', as he was known, had joined the Air Battalion on 3 April 1911. He participated in the 1911 army manoeuvres, piloting a box-kite biplane. On the formation of the RFC in 1912 he became Adjutant with the headquarters at Farnborough. He was regarded as one of the finest fliers of the day and, on 14 February 1912, was awarded the Mortimer Singer Prize for the longest flight by an officer of the army. Flying a Nieuport monoplane, and carrying a passenger, he flew 249½ miles. Jimmy McCudden, later a famous fighter pilot and VC but who was then serving as an air mechanic, had this to say of him in his

B H Barrington-Kennett.

autobiography *Five Years in the Royal Flying Corps*:

> *The R.F.C. at this time was roughly eight hundred N.C.O.'s and men strong, and about forty pilots, and despite, or perhaps owing to its lack of numbers, it was very efficient and highly disciplined. This was due to the fact that the original N.C.O.s of the R.F.C. were largely transfers from the Guards, the Adjutant, Lieutenant Barrington-Kennett, being a Guardsman. The Royal Engineers had also contributed largely to the personnel. What accounted for this excellent state of affairs was that the R.F.C. tried to live up to Barrington-Kennett's vow that the R.F.C. should combine the smartness of the Guards with the efficiency of the Sappers, and it was actually true of the pre-war R.F.C.*

The efficient way the RFC campaigned in the early days of the war was largely due to 'B-K's organisational skills and his tireless efforts. On 7 February 1915 he was confined to bed with influenza and then spent three days in hospital, following which he went on leave. On recovery he was told by doctors that office work was not good for him, so he applied to return to the Grenadiers, though he had been offered command of a squadron in the RFC.

On 18 May 1915 the Grenadier Guards, together with the Irish Guards and Canadians, attacked the German positions in the Le Touret area. The attack failed due to the flatness of the countryside, swept by machine gun fire and enfilading artillery shells. Casualties amounted to fifteen killed, four missing and 71 wounded. One of the fatal casualties was Major B H Barrington-Kennett.

When Maurice Baring heard of his death he wrote:

But of all the bitter losses one had to bear throughout the war, it was, with one exception this particular loss I felt most, minded most, resented most and found most difficult to accept.

He was not an old friend of mine. I had not seen him before the war. But he was bound up with every moment of my life during the first months of the war, and I had got to know him intimately and to admire him more than others and to delight in his company more than in that of others. He had left the Flying Corps, and I should probably not have seen much more of him, unless, as would have perhaps been possible later, he had returned to it. But when this particular piece of news came I felt the taste of the war turn bitter indeed, and apart from any personal feelings, one rebelled against the waste which had deprived, first the Flying Corps and then the Army, of the services of so noble a character. He was the most completely unselfish man I ever met: a compound of loyalty and generosity and a gay and keen interest in everything life had to offer.

The Barrington-Kennett family suffered terribly in the First World War, as of four sons they had already lost one in September 1914 and were destined to lose a third in 1916 (*Somme*, page 31).

Continue ahead on the D171 and at the roundabout turn left for Béthune. Pass over the canal and at the next roundabout take the D937 to Hazebrouck and Dunkirk. Go left on the D182 towards Gonnehem and Chocques. At the crossroads go ahead down the Rue de Blanc Sabot. The derelict Chateau de Werppe will appear on the right. Turn right towards it and the aerodrome was in the field on the left.

Chocques Aerodrome

The site of this aerodrome is marked by the distinctive Chateau de Werppe adjacent to it. The building has been derelict for years but, like so many unused structures in France, has neither been demolished nor badly vandalised. In the early days it was known as Gonneham but it is more familiarly referred to as Chocques.

The first squadron to occupy the field was No. 3, who arrived on 24 November 1914. Their arrival was described by Jimmy McCudden again:

About the end of November No. 3 Squadron moved to an aerodrome at Gonneham, near Chocques. We arrived here and

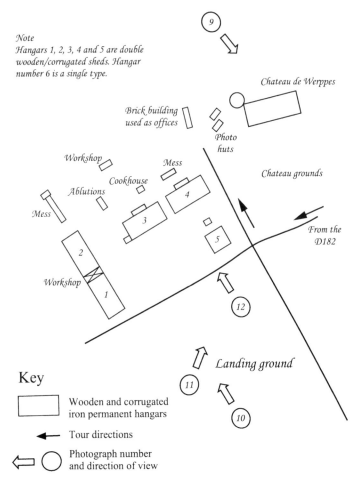

Note
Hangars 1, 2, 3, 4 and 5 are double
wooden/corrugated sheds. Hangar
number 6 is a single type.

Chateau de Werppes

Brick building
used as offices

Photo
huts

Workshop

Mess

Cookhouse

Chateau grounds

Ablutions

Mess

4

Mess

3

5

From the
D182

2

Workshop

1

12

Landing ground

11

10

Key

Wooden and corrugated
iron permanent hangars

Tour directions

Photograph number
and direction of view

Picture No. 9: The aerodrome and chateau looking southeast in 2001.

AERODROME

FROM
D 182

CHATEAU
DE
WERPPE

HANGARS

Picture No. 10: The aerodrome, probably in 1917, looking northwest. Attention seems to be surrounding a visiting Nieuport Scout.

found the proposed aerodrome was a beet field. Some Indian cavalry had a roller and were attempting to level the uneven ground, while every available man in the Squadron turned out to be marched up and down the field to harden the ground and to press down the beet roots. We spent a whole afternoon doing this, and although the ground was very soft it was good enough to land upon when we had finished.

The weather at this time was very wet indeed, and practically as soon as we had erected all our hangars a gale would arrive and blow every one of them down. I cannot attempt to describe the state of things under these circumstances. Rain pouring in torrents, wind howling like mad, and all the hangars level with the ground flapping about the machines.

To make things more cheerful, there were deep ditches around the hangars to catch the water, and every minute or so one heard a loud splash, to the accompaniment of curses and oaths, as some unfortunate mechanic fell into one of these drainage pools.

We had nothing like enough hangar accommodation for all our Squadron machines, so at night every machine that could not be put in a hangar had to be tied down in the open day and night in the depth of winter. I hardly need mention that an 80 h.p. Gnôme Blériot

Picture No. 11: The Blériots of 3 Squadron at Chocques in the wimter of 1914/15.

10 Squadron on parade in 1916.

that was sodden with water, and carrying a passenger and full war load, took some getting out of Gonneham aerodrome with its bad approaches. When we got settled a little here, about twelve tons of cinders were deposited on the aerodrome every day in order to make it possible for our under-powered and heavily-loaded machines to land and get off from it.

Our aerodrome at Gonneham was only seven miles from the nearest part of the line, and in the clear spring evenings we could follow with our own eyesight our machines until they were "Archied" over the trenches. On some evenings we could see a river of white shell-bursts, from south of Armentières almost down to Lens.

The chateau during the First World War with an RFC workshop lorry parked alongside.

Picture No. 12: Armstrong Whitworth FK8, or Big Ack B5772. The white line on the lower longeron was 10 Squadron's marking.

No. 3 Squadron occupied the aerodrome until June 1915. Other units based here were 4, 10 (who were stationed on it for over two years), 16, and 42 Squadrons. At the beginning of the Battle of the Somme in July 1916, the chateau was the headquarters of I Brigade RFC.

The Portuguese Flying Corps

It is a well-known fact that the Portuguese army fought on the Western Front but what is not so well-known is that they had a number of fliers as well.

The British Mission with the Portuguese Division advised British Army GHQ of the Portuguese government's desire to have a flying corps as part of their expeditionary force. In late December 1916, a party of Portuguese officers, including five aviators, arrived in the British First Army area. Initially they were going to be spread amongst a number of units but, in the event, were all sent to 10 Squadron RFC at Chocques, where they arrived in January 1917.

The pilots were Lieutenants Oscar Monteiro Torres, Antonio de Sousa Maya and José Barbosa dos Santos Leite. The fourth was Second Lieutenant Alberto Lelo Portella. The party was completed by an engineer officer, Second Lieutenant Joao Branco.

Torres, Maya and Portella had learned to fly in England and obtained their Royal Aero Club certificates, whilst Leite had had his tuition in France. All had completed about 100 hours flying. Though they were pilots, the whole of January was spent observing and not being allowed to fly. The Portuguese had requested enough machines to establish one flight and a headquarters. In addition they needed transport and other equipment. The RFC were unable to meet the request for, understandably, they had few enough resources for themselves.

By December 1917 the Portuguese had ten pilots and twenty-nine mechanics, all trained in France. There were 58 pilots and mechanics training in France and fifteen observers under tuition in the UK. At home they had another 70 or so personnel.

In December 1917, Leite, Maya and Portella joined the French fighter unit *Spa* 124. This had been the original *Lafayette Escadrille* but in early 1918 its American personnel had transferred to the US air service (*Somme*, page 119). Leite and Maya returned to the Portuguese army in April 1918 but Portella remained until July and was awarded the *Croix de Guerre* and the *Légion d'Honneur*. He died on 10 October 1949.

Leite, who was born on 21 March 1884 at Penacova-Coimbra, Portugal, had learned to fly at Pau, in France. He died in a mid-air collision at Alverca, Portugal on 30 November 1928, as a major.

Maya, born in Oporto on 1 October 1888, had learned to fly at the Ruffy-Baumann School at Hendon. Staying in military flying after the war he was promoted to colonel in 1937 and passed into the reserve in 1941. He died on 11 June 1969.

The fourth pilot who served with 10 Squadron is of particular interest.

Oscar Monteiro Torres

Torres was born on 26 March 1889 at S Paulo de Luanda, Angola. He obtained his Royal Aero Club certificate, No. 3013, on a Caudron biplane at the Ruffy-Baumann School, Hendon on 2 June 1916. He spoke both French and English. After his month flying in the Armstrong Whitworth FK8 or Big Ack, as it was known, he also flew with the French, but with *Spa* 65, who were operating Spads. On 19 November 1917 Torres, by now promoted to captain, was shot down on the German side and died of his wounds. He was subsequently awarded the French *Légion d'Honneur* and *Croix de Guerre* and promoted

Oscar Monteiro Torres.

Rudolf Windisch in Torres' Spad. The machine has been painted red but the *Spa* 65 unit marking has been retained.

to major by the Portuguese. Torres was the sixth victory of Rudolf Windisch of *Jasta* 32. His machine was captured intact and flown by Windisch, though there is some doubt as to whether he flew it on operations. Windisch was shot down within French lines on 27 May 1918, as commander of *Jasta* 66. It was believed he was still alive, and so his recommendation for the *Pour le Mérite* was approved. However, no trace of him was ever found.

Torres was buried by the Germans in Laon but in June 1930 his body was returned to Portugal and interred in Lisbon.

Return to the crossroads and turn right on the D181 towards Oblinghem into of Chocques. At the crossroads turn right into the centre. As the road bears left turn right into Rue de Gonnehem, then take the first right into Rue des Martyrs to the cemetery.

Chocques Military Cemetery

The Chocques area remained in Allied hands throughout the war and the village was at one time the headquarters of I Corps. No. 1 Casualty Clearing Station was situated here from January 1915 until April 1918. The burials in the cemetery (14/18) are casualties brought back from the front who later died of their wounds. This is reflected in the low proportion of unknown graves - only 134 out of a total of 1,800.

There are 47 flyer's graves here and the numbers are representative of the units in the area. There are twenty casualties from 10 Squadron, eleven from 3 Squadron and nine from 4 Squadron, all based at Chocques. In addition there are five from 2 Squadron at nearby Hesdigneul aerodrome (see page 105)

The first grave (I B10) we have come to visit is in the second row in on the left from the entrance, and is the result of a terrible accident at Chocques aerodrome on 12 March 1915.

A Disastrous Bomb Accident (I B10)

Jimmy McCudden, who was serving in 3 Squadron at the time, wrote of the incident:

We were now receiving fairly large size bombs for disposal. One type, which was painted red, weighed ten pounds, and had a small parachute attached to give it directional stability; it was called a shrapnel bomb. Another new type, which was called the Mélinite bomb, weighed twenty-six pounds, and had a striker in the nose to detonate it. This bomb was really a converted French shell, and was afterwards condemned as being highly unsafe. I mention these bombs because they were our early attempts at producing this very necessary adjunct to aerial warfare.

About 5 p.m. on March 12th I had just seen Captain Conran and Mr. Pinney off on a Morane, and on my way back to my flight shed passed Captain Cholmondeley and his Morane outside "A" Flight sheds. The machine was then being loaded with six of the Mélinite bombs which have already been mentioned. I had just got to my flight sheds when "crump-crump" came two explosions in quick succession, and I distinctly felt the displacement of air. I turned round and saw Captain Cholmondeley's Morane on fire from wing-tip to wing-tip.

Two bombs had exploded during the loading process. I ran over to render assistance and found about a dozen men lying around the Morane, all badly mutilated. Owing to the Morane being on fire and still more bombs being in the machine we got away the wounded quickly.

I well remember the little band of helpers who assisted to get the living away from the burning wreckage at the imminent risk of their own lives. Lieutenants Pretyman, Blackburn, Cleaver and Sergeant Burns were the leaders of the party.

Major Salmond had now arrived and ordered everyone away from the machine, he himself remaining by the wreck - a splendid example of coolness that still further increased our great respect of our Commanding Officer.

This was a very bad day for our Squadron, for in this accident we had eleven killed and two wounded, among whom were some very experienced and valuable members of No. 3 Squadron. Captain Cholmondeley was one of the best-liked officers in the Squadron, as well as one of our finest pilots, and Flight-Sergeants Costigan and Bowyer, two of our earliest N.C.O.'s, were also among the dead. The accident had a generally depressing effect, noticeable for days in the Squadron.

I do not think that the cause of the mishap was ever really discovered. It was surmised that during the loading of the bombs a safety wire was accidentally pulled. However, the Squadron settled down to its work again, but we who had seen the accident can never forget it; at least I never can.

In fact eight people were killed in the explosion, comprising Captain Cholmendeley and seven other ranks.

Captain Reginald Harold Cholmondelely (I B10)

The Commonwealth War Graves Commission policy is that there is no segregation by rank, and a lowly private can be buried alongside a general. However, at certain cemeteries that were used by hospitals, field

ambulances or casualty clearing stations you find that there are separate rows for officers and other ranks. This is the case at Chocques, where all the officer casualties of 10 Squadron are buried together. Despite being killed in the same incident, Cholmondeley is buried in a different row from the other ranks who lost their lives in the explosion.

Born on 26 September 1889 in Hatfield, Cholmondeley attended Eton from September

R H Cholmondeley. 1902 until March 1907 and then was tutored privately. He was commissioned into the Rifle Brigade in April 1909. While serving with 1/Rifle Brigade at Colchester he learned to fly at his own expense with the Grahame-White School, Hendon. He obtained his flying certificate, No.271, on 13 August 1912, on a Grahame-White biplane, having already applied to join the RFC in May 1912, to which he was attached on 19 January 1913.

Cholmondeley had gone to France with the RFC in August 1914 as a flight commander in the aircraft park. After an aeroplane accident in December he spent some time convalescing in Nice.

The graves of the other ranks involved in this incident are in a line on the left at the back of the cemetery and have two stone memorials behind them.

Flight Sergeant Joseph Lester Costigan

Born at Putney in 1889, Costigan had been an electrician before joining up in July 1909 and enlisted as a gunner. In June 1912 he transferred from the artillery to the newly formed RFC as a second class air mechanic. Promotion to sergeant followed in July 1913 and he went to France with 3 Squadron in August 1914. His RFC number was 194.

Corporal Oliver Francis Vernon Bowyer

Born in Bracknell and one of three brothers, Bowyer joined the RFC on 6 February 1913, having been a draper's clerk in civilian life. He was aged twenty years and two months. Promotion to First Class Air Mechanic was promulgated on 1 November 1913 and to corporal on 15 February 1915, shortly before he was killed. His RFC number was 582.

First Class Air Mechanic Wilfred Barker

Barker, born in St Andrews, Derby was aged eighteen years and three months when he joined up. Attested on 14 January 1913, he had been a mechanic in civilian life and had served with the North Midland Howitzer Brigade, RFA. He was promoted to first class air mechanic on 1 July 1914 and went to France the following month with 3 Squadron. His RFC number was 534.

First Class Air Mechanic Albert Thomas James Morgan
Morgan had served as a lance corporal in 2/King's Royal Rifle Corps, before transferring to the RFC on 12 April 1913. He went to France on 13 August 1914 as a first class air mechanic. His RFC number was 872.

First Class Air Mechanic George Cook
A signwriter and painter, Cook was born in Windsor and had joined the RFC on 7 February 1913. He may very well have been friends with Bowyer, as both of them had served in 4/Royal Berkshire Regiment and been attested into the RFC on the same day. Cook was promoted to first class air mechanic on 15 September 1914, having gone out to France in August with 3 Squadron. His RFC number was 589.

First Class Air Mechanic Arthur Hugo Charles Cuff
Born in St Peters, Bournemouth, he was twenty years old when he joined the RFC, having served with the RGA (Territorial Force). Arriving at South Farnborough on 17 April 1914, he travelled with 3 Squadron to France on 13 August. His RFC number was 1192.

First Class Air Mechanic Samuel James Tugwell
With an RFC number of 1934, Tugwell was the only person killed in this incident who was not a pre-war regular. Born in Eastbourne, he was aged twenty when he joined the RFC on 28 October 1914, and had been an apprentice with the Eastbourne Motor Cab Company for five years. He was promoted to first class air mechanic on 1 March 1915, only days before he was killed.

Also injured in the accident was Second Class Air Mechanic S Bird (1171), who was later promoted to flight sergeant. He later served for three years in the Middle East and India, before being discharged in June 1920 with a disability pension.

A second airman wounded was Second Class Air Mechanic Ernest Welsh (2643). Born in 1893 he had been a fitter and turner before joining the RFC. He had injuries to the face and arm but returned to 3 Squadron. He served with the unit from January 1915 until January 1919 and was discharged in December 1922.

William Henry Burns who was involved in the rescue of the wounded, unfortunately died of wounds on 6 October 1915, after having acted as a signaller for over-flying RFC machines. He left a widow, and is buried at Étaples Military Cemetery.

George Bernard Ward, MC and bar (V C4)

G B Ward.

The next grave we are visiting is one of the many 10 Squadron casualties and is situated near to the Cross of Sacrifice.

George, the son of David Ward of Lower Hall, Foxearth, Essex, was born on 18 August 1891. A second lieutenant in 9/North Staffordshire Regiment, he joined the RFC at South Farnborough on 13 September 1915. He had earned his civilian ticket, No.1590, the previous month, with the London and Provincial School at Hendon. Further military flying training followed at the Central Flying School and No. 1 Reserve Aeroplane Squadron, before joining 2 Squadron in France on 19 February 1916. They were based at Hesdigneul, southwest of Bethune (see page 105) and were operating the ubiquitous BE2 on army tasks. In only two and a half months he was promoted to flight commander and in December 1916 further advancement followed. He was sent from 2 Squadron direct to No. 10 as squadron commander. They also were operating the BE2 but in early June 1917 began to replace these with the Armstrong Whitworth FK8, or Big Ack as it was known. Surprisingly, only five squadrons on the Western Front were fully equipped with this type, which was well liked and in many ways a better machine than the RE8.

On 21 September 1917, Ward and his observer, Second Lieutenant William Archibald Campbell, took off on a late morning photo reconnaissance patrol. Ground observers saw them in combat with four enemy fighters. The machine crashed on landing and Ward was killed. Campbell was taken to hospital with a compound fracture of the skull and later died of his injuries. The observer's standby control lever was found in its socket, so it seems likely that Ward may have been wounded and incapacitated, with Campbell having to fly the aeroplane. Possibly the observer lost control during the attempted landing, or fatal combat damage caused the machine to crash.

Campbell, who was originally commissioned into the 7/Yorkshire Regiment, had been attached to the RFC in May 1917 and been posted to 10 Squadron on 26 June. He is buried alongside his squadron commander in grave V C5.

Return to the Rue de Gonnehem and turn right. Follow the D70 out of the village for Lapugnoy. Continue through Lapugnoy and turn right for Allouagne and La Roseraie. Up the hill turn left at the green War Graves Commission sign to the cemetery.

Lapugnoy Military Cemetery

This cemetery (14/20) contains three particularly interesting aviation related graves, the first of which is situated at the far end of the second row on the right as the visitor enters the cemetery. Altogether there are 54 flying casualties buried here, of which twenty-three are from 25 Squadron and six from 43 Squadron. Both units were based at nearby Lozinghem.

The first burials in the cemetery were made in late 1915 but its heaviest use was in the Battle of Arras, which began in April 1917, when casualties were brought in from nearby casualty clearing stations. There is now a total of about 1,300 dead commemorated here.

Brigadier-General Gordon Strachey Shephard (VI B15)

Shephard has the dubious distinction of being the highest ranking officer in the British flying services to be killed during the Great War.

Born on 9 July 1885 in Madras, the son of Sir Horatio Shephard, a Judge in the High Court. The family returned to England in 1901 and set up home in Montague Square, London. Educated at Eton, Gordon passed the Military College course in 1904 and was promoted to lieutenant two years later.

His great passion was sailing, and it was during cruises round the Baltic that he took photographs of the German coast, which almost certainly were passed on to the relevant intelligence departments in the War Office. It has been alleged that Shephard was the basis for Erskine Childers central character in his spy novel *Riddle of the Sands*, though this is unlikely. During 1914 Shephard aided Childers in landing arms in Ireland for the Southern Irish Volunteers. Fortunately, war intervened because this incident could have had a very serious effect on his career. Shephard learned to fly initially at Hendon, gaining his Royal Aero Club 'ticket', No. 215, on 14 May 1912 and in July was ordered to join the RFC. In the 1913 army manoeuvres he flew as a pilot and observer. At the outbreak of war he went to France as a flight commander with 4 Squadron and made his first reconnaissance on 22 August. In November 1914 Shephard returned home and

Brigadier-General G
S Shephard.

98

was given command of No. 1 Reserve Aeroplane Squadron. During March 1915 he took command of 6 Squadron in France. He had three exceptional flight commanders, who were all to make their mark. They were Lanoe Hawker (*Somme*, page 81), Louis Strange (*Cambrai*, page 31) and B T James (*Ypres*, page 40)

In December 1915 Shephard returned to England, promoted to lieutenant-colonel and given command of 8 Wing, but at the end of January 1916 returned to France in charge of 12 Wing. They were to be heavily involved in the Battle of the Somme, which began on 1 July. A year later Shephard took temporary command of III Brigade and the following month was promoted to temporary Brigadier-General and placed in charge of I Brigade.

Shephard was no chateau general and not only flew himself round his squadrons but also crossed the lines to see the situation for himself. His brigade headquarters was on the aerodrome at Bruay and William MacLanachan, in his book *Fighter Pilot*, wrote of an amusing but potentially disastrous incident:

> The ground by this time was almost black and, with my nose well down, I flew with all speed to Bruay.
>
> Having no lights to illuminate my instruments, and failing to see more than the dim outlines of the hangars, I made a very fast landing far out on the aerodrome. In the darkness I failed to see another machine standing in the middle of the landing-stretch and, catching sight of it only just in time, I had to put on full right rudder to avoid crashing into it. Purely by luck my Nieuport fell back on her wheels after attempting to pirouette on her wingtip, and as I climbed out hurriedly General Shephard and two mechanics ran up to me to see if I were hurt.
>
> Our youthful Brigadier-General (he was only thirty-one) explained that he had landed seven or eight minutes previously and had 'lost' his engine. While the mechanics were attempting

Shephard's original grave marker.

to restart it they had heard the sound of my engine, "Run like Hell, Sir," one of the mechanics had said and, jumping out of his machine, the General had 'run like Hell' out of danger's way, accompanied by the mechanics.

Such incidents cemented the camaraderie that existed in the R.F.C. Our Brigadier very frequently crossed the lines with us on special missions, and whenever an attack was in progress his Nieuport was to be seen hovering about, watching what was happening or taking his part in whatever engagements required his assistance.

Unfortunately, Shephard's habit of flying visits was to be the cause of his demise. On 19 January 1918 he took off from Bruay in his Nieuport scout to pay a call on his units based at nearby Auchel. For reasons unknown, he spun into the ground on the edge of Auchel aerodrome, and was removed to hospital, where he died of his injuries.

In his book *Years of Combat* Sholto Douglas (later Marshal of the Royal Air Force Lord Douglas of Kirtleside) had this to say about Shephard:

There was one other man under whom we came to serve at that time who was also to provide me with a lesson in this matter of leadership. We were in the First Brigade of the Flying Corps, which was commanded by Gordon Shephard, a Brigadier who, for all his exalted rank, was only about thirty-five years of age. One of the earliest of the pilots in the Flying Corps, he was somewhat vacuous in appearance with a receding chin and afflicted with a slight lisp - physically a colourless personality - but that was the only thing about him that was lacking in colour.

Although he was not a good pilot, Gordon Shephard's mind was of a brilliance that would undoubtedly have led to his becoming in time one of the great leaders in the Air Force; but that poor flying of his brought about his death in an accident before the end of the war, and so his name came to play only a minor role in the history of flying.

Harold Richard Johnson (I E9)

The next grave we are visiting is towards the rear of the cemetery near the beginning of one of the long rows and is very obvious with its large civilian headstone.

The first time I visited this cemetery it was specifically to see Gordon Shephard's grave but my eye was drawn to a non-standard headstone in the distance. These are

H R Johnson.

Morane Type LA 5178 of 3 Squadron.

uncommon and this one particularly so, as it belongs to a flyer.

Johnson was born on 18 December 1888 and came from Tonbridge in Kent. He attended Sir Andrew Judd's Commercial School in Tonbridge and served in the West Kent Yeomanry for six years. Prior to being commissioned in May 1915 he spent three months in the ranks. Though he had taken his 'ticket', No. 703, on 11 December 1913, Johnson did not join the RFC until May 1915. After military flying training at 2 RAS, Brooklands and 15 Squadron, he was posted to 3 Squadron on 11 August 1915. They were based at Lozinghem, quite near this cemetery, and had Moranes of different types.

On 19 January 1916 Johnson and his observer W S Fielding-Johnson took off in Morane 5099 and crashed for unknown reasons.

He must have been held in some regard for his brother officers to erect this headstone in his memory.

The non-standard headstone on H R Johnson's grave.

William Spurrett Fielding-Johnson

Born on 26 September 1892 Fielding-Johnson had joined the RFC in 1915, after service in the Leicestershire Yeomanry, where he was awarded an MC. He joined 3 Squadron in late 1915 and was injured in the crash with Johnson. After pilot training, he joined the famous 56 Squadron on 11 October 1917, where he met Jimmy McCudden, whom he had known during their time together in 3 Squadron. While with 56 Squadron Fielding-Johnson earned a bar to his MC, having claimed six victories. He had also twice been Mentioned in Despatches. In the Second World War he served as a gunner in the RAF, being shot down and having to take to his parachute. He was awarded a DFC and died in 1953.

W S Fielding-Johnson wearing his observer's wing and Military Cross ribbon.

The Battle of the Knights? (I F39)

While standing next to Johnson's grave, in the distance I could see a solitary German headstone and, as my chum Jim Davies and I walked towards it, I remarked to him that almost certainly it must be another flyer! And sure enough it was, and an unusual one too. The grave is further along to the left in the next row.

Lord Doune and Georg Wilhelm von Saalfeld

Francis Douglas Stuart, Lord Doune was born on 10 July 1892 and was the eldest son of the 17th Earl of Moray. He was educated at Eton College and then Trinity College, Cambridge from 1911 to 1914. He was commissioned into the Scottish Horse but in August 1915 joined the RFC. After training at Montrose and CFS, he joined 25 Squadron on 2 November 1915. The squadron moved to France in February 1916 and on 1 April set up their base at Lozinghem. They were to remain there until October 1917. Their equipment was the RAF FE2b and this machine, together with the DH2, put to an end the dominance of the Fokker *Eindecker*, and the so-called Fokker Scourge.

Lord Doune.

Barely a month after their arrival at the front 25 Squadron scored a notable victory. On the morning of 29 April three FEs took off on a patrol and at 11,000 feet in the Loos area they spotted an *Eindecker*. Doune and his observer, Second Lieutenant R V Walker, recorded the incident in their combat report:

> At 11 a.m. when two miles over the lines between Hulluch and La Bassée, a Fokker was sighted about 2,000 feet below. The F.E. dived at it and the Observer opened fire at 80 yards, when the Fokker manoeuvred to get behind the F.E.s tail. The machines flew round each other several times; the Fokker twice succeeded in firing at the F.E. from behind, but was soon shaken off. The third time the two machines approached each other, the pilot and observer were both firing at the Fokker, when, as he passed within 20 feet over the F.E. one wing was seen to crumple up and the Fokker fell to earth in a spinning nose dive, drifting with the wind behind our lines. It appears to Lord Doune that pieces of one plane fell clear of the machine which seemed to be falling with only one plane.
>
> The observer fired four drums and the pilot one.

Unteroffizier Georg *Freiherr* von Saalfeld

Their opponent was the elder son of the elder Prince Ernst of Saxe-Meiningen, one of the Thuringian states. A younger brother had been killed in Russia during 1915. Von Saalfeld had lost a leg as the result of an accident when aged fifteen but, nevertheless, was able to complete his flying training. He was posted to a *Kampfeinzitzer-Kommando (KEK)*, attached to *Feldflieger-Abteilung (FA)* 18. He had only been with them a month before he was killed.

In 1929 Lord Doune was staying in a hotel in Freiburg, having medical treatment, when he was visited by Prince Ernst's youngest son. Ernst and he had been in touch through a mutual friend and Doune was able to reassure the family about the circumstances of Georg's death. He told them their son had not been shot down in flames and that the head and face were untouched, and in fact his expression was *calm, satisfied and rather cheerful*. It was believed that von Saalfeld had died of bullet wounds in the air. They were also grateful that Doune had had their son's body brought back and that he was given a funeral the same as a British officer would receive.

For this action both Doune and Walker received the MC. On 16 June 1916 Doune was wounded and in

103

Georg von Saalfeld.

The plate removed from von Saalfeld's Fokker recording its number 434/15. This is now on display in the museum at Edinburgh Castle.

A permit dated 17 March 1916 at Mannheim, signed by von Saalfeld authorising him to fly an unarmed *Eindecker*.

October was posted to Home Defence, joining 50 (HD) Squadron as a flight commander. He held various staff appointments but relinquished his commission due to ill-health in March 1920. He succeeded his father in 1930 as 18th Earl of Moray but his health never really recovered, and he died the day before his 51st birthday on 9 July 1943.

Robert Verschoyle Walker

Walker was born on 18 December 1893 in Falcaragh, Donegal. He served in the ranks of the Leinster Regiment during the second half of 1915 but was then commissioned into the Connaught Rangers. He transferred to the RFC in April 1916. While flying over the lines on 7 June Walker was wounded by shrapnel, which broke his lower jaw. He was discharged from hospital in August with two large lumps still in his jaw, as the doctors had decided not to remove them.

Having trained as a pilot, he misjudged a night landing at Hounslow on 31 October 1917 and crashed. He was thrown out and concussed, receiving injuries to his face and legs. On 17 April 1919 he was transferred to the unemployed list.

Return to the D70 and turn right to a roundabout, where you take a left turn on the D188 to Bruay-la-Buissiere. At the N41 turn left towards Béthune and the A26. Continue over two roundabouts and after the Hesdigneul-les-Béthune village sign turn right into Rue Maurice Fardoux. This housing estate is where Hesdigneul aerodrome was located.

Hesdigneul Aerodrome

The area around Lens and Béthune is heavily industrialised and quite densely populated by French standards. The next two places we are visiting have largely disappeared under housing and a sports arena but they are

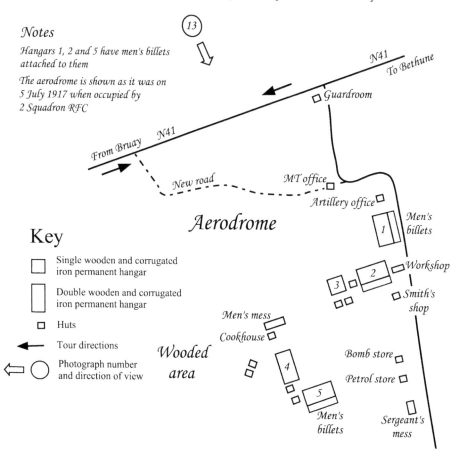

Notes

Hangars 1, 2 and 5 have men's billets attached to them

The aerodrome is shown as it was on 5 July 1917 when occupied by 2 Squadron RFC

13

N41 To Bethune

Guardroom

From Bruay   N41

New road   MT office

Artillery office

Aerodrome

Men's billets

1

Workshop

2

3   Smith's shop

Men's mess

Cookhouse

Wooded area

4   Bomb store

Petrol store

5

Men's billets   Sergeant's mess

Key

☐ Single wooden and corrugated iron permanent hangar

▯ Double wooden and corrugated iron permanent hangar

☐ Huts

← Tour directions

⇐ ◯ Photograph number and direction of view

Picture No. 13: Hesdigneul in 2003 view looking southeast.

well worth seeing as important events occurred at both sites.

No. 2 Squadron RFC arrived at Hesdigneul on 30 June 1915 and remained until June 1918, an unprecedented time to be based in one place, as most units were moved about fairly frequently. The only other squadron that seems to have been stationed here was 21 Squadron, who occupied it for only a week in late October 1918.

Big Ack C8632 '14' of 2 Squadron. This was a veteran machine, serving with the unit from 2 June 1918 until 25 January 1919.

Alan Arnett McLeod VC

P E Butcher, an NCO with 2 Squadron, who had served with it in France since the outbreak of war, wrote in his autobiography, *Skill and Devotion:*

Alan McLeod VC.

Towards the end of 1917, a very young Canadian officer, in fact only seventeen years of age (sic), named Alan McLeod joined the Squadron. He reminded me very much of McCudden and would walk around and get into conversation with the mechanics, wanting to know all about the peculiarities of the F.K.8 which he was going to fly. We all liked him as he was an officer full of life and, for a lad of his age, knew no fear. At first he was not keen about the Ack W, as the machines were termed by us, but he soon got the hang of this heavy reconnaissance bomber. It seemed he had heard such glowing reports about the famous No. 2 Squadron, that he had asked to be posted to us, where, he told me, he put all his confidence in his N.C.O. and mechanics. He was always wanting to know all about the Squadron's history and past doings, I remember.

The general consensus of opinion amongst us all was that he was going to get somewhere by his keenness, and almost before we knew it, he and his observer, Lieut. Camber, had brought down a Fokker, the first to fall to an F.K.8. Later this was confirmed by the Balloon Observers, but he seemed cut out for something bigger, and the New Year was to prove us right.

By now my health and nerves were beginning to suffer and give trouble under strain, so it was with mixed feelings that I found, posted in orders, that I was to return home with effect from March 21st.

One of the first people I told of my going was young Lieut. McLeod who wanted to know exactly how long I had been on active service. When I told him three years and seven months, and that I had seen service all along the Western Front from Ypres to the Somme, he was most interested, shaking my hand and wishing me the best of luck. Six days after I had returned to England, as I heard later, he had earned the Victoria Cross.

McLeod was born in Stonewall, Manitoba on 20 April 1899, the son of a doctor. Keen on the military from an early age he tried to join the Fort Garry Horse, a local militia unit, but failed due to his youth. Once having attained the minimum military enlistment age, he applied for pilot training in the RFC. His flying tuition was carried out in Canada and he was awarded RFC 'wings' on 31 July 1917. He sailed for the UK and finished training at Winchester. His great desire was to fly fighters but in the event he was sent to 2 Squadron at Hesdigneul on 29 November 1917. Though disappointed at operating slow two-seaters, at least he was on active service. He acquired the nickname of 'Babe', despite being six feet two inches tall, and soon demonstrated he was a 'fire eater'. The duties of a two-seater squadron were conscientiously performed but he would frequently finish off a patrol by strafing German ground targets, flying his Big Ack like a fighter. On 19 December 1917 he attacked a formation of eight German scouts and J O Comber, his observer, sent one down out of control. On 14 January 1918 he and his observer shot down a kite balloon and an enemy scout that attacked them.

On 21 March the great German offensive commenced and the RFC were soon flying endless sorties, trying to stem the advancing enemy. Six days later McLeod, and Second Lieutenant A W Hammond, left on a patrol to bomb German troop concentrations in the Bray-sur-Somme area but due to poor weather were forced to land at Avesnes-le-Comte to refuel (see page 154). After lunch they set off again but the weather was still as bad. After two fruitless hours, they were about to return to their aerodrome when a kite balloon was spotted. They were about to attack it when a Fokker Triplane was observed, and this was attacked instead and sent down to crash.

Unfortunately, they were then pounced upon by eight machines from *Jagdgeschwader* I. Both men were wounded and their machine set on fire by *Leutnant* Hans Kirschstein of *Jasta* 6. McLeod flew the aeroplane balanced on the left lower wing to avoid the flames, whilst Hammond perched on top of the fuselage. The Big Ack eventually crashed in No Man's Land. McLeod pulled Hammond from the wreckage and dragged him into the British front line trenches. When they eventually received medical attention, it was found that Hammond was wounded in six places, including a shattered leg and McLeod had five wounds.

Evacuated to England, McLeod was in a critical state for some weeks and his father travelled from Canada to be with him. He recovered sufficiently to travel to Buckingham Palace to be invested with his Victoria Cross by King George V on 4 September 1918.

The citation for his VC reads:

> *Whilst flying with his observer (Lieutenant A.W.Hammond, MC), attacking hostile formations by bombs and machine gun fire, he was assailed at a height of 5,000 feet by eight enemy triplanes which dived at him from all directions, firing from their front guns. By skilful manoeuvring he enabled his observer to fire bursts at each machine in turn, shooting three of them down out of control. By this time Lieutenant McLeod had received five wounds, and whilst continuing the engagement a bullet penetrated his petrol tank and*

set the machine on fire. He then climbed out on to the left bottom plane, controlling the machine from the side of the fuselage, and by side-slipping steeply kept the flames to one side, thus enabling the observer to continue firing until the ground was reached. The observer had been wounded six times when the machine crashed in No Man's Land, and 2nd Lieutenant McLeod, notwithstanding his own wounds, dragged him away from the burning wreckage at great personal risk from heavy machine gun fire from the enemy's lines. This very gallant pilot was again wounded by a bomb whilst engaged in this act of rescue, but he persevered until he had placed Lieutenant Hammond in comparative safety, before falling himself from exhaustion and loss of blood.

At the end of September he was well enough to return to Canada, where he seemed to be making a steady recovery. Tragically, in his weakened state, he fell victim to the influenza epidemic and died on 6 November, just five days before the Armistice and still aged only nineteen years.

Arthur William Hammond

Hammond arrived at No. 1 School of Military Aeronautics on 2 May 1917 and after wireless and observer training at Brooklands, went overseas and was posted to 2 Squadron on 10 September. He was wounded on 3 December 1917 but remained with the unit. During his service with the squadron he was awarded an MC and bar. After his wounding with McLeod, he spent months in hospital and eventually his leg was amputated. He relinquished his commission due to ill-health on 6 September 1919 and later migrated to Winnipeg, where he spent the rest of his days.

McLeod and Hammond were Hans Kirschstein's second victory. He had a distinguished career, including the award of the *Pour le Mérite*, before being killed in a flying accident on 16 July 1918. For further details of his career see *Airfields and Airmen, Verdun*, Laon Bousson German Cemetery.

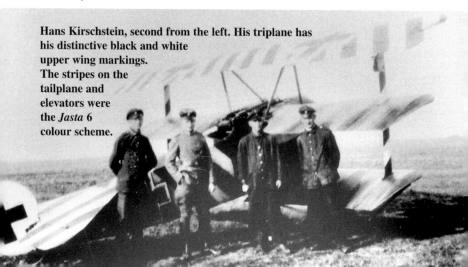

Hans Kirschstein, second from the left. His triplane has his distinctive black and white upper wing markings. The stripes on the tailplane and elevators were the *Jasta* 6 colour scheme.

King George V's visit

Another interesting, but perhaps less glorious, incident occurred here during an inspection by the King.

Again it was recalled by P E Butcher in *Skill and Devotion*:

> *Shortly after this I was recalled from the forward area and the next day we had the honour of a visit from His Majesty King George V. After inspecting the Brigade of Guards, he rode on to the Hesdigneul airfield and inspected us before congratulating all concerned on the good work we were doing.*
>
> *"Three cheers for His Majesty" the C.O.s voice rang out at the end of the King's words. At the first roar I noticed that almost imperceptible backward movement of the rear hooves of the royal mount, which always marks a frightened horse. Then, before any of us realised what was happening, the animal reared up, the immaculate white picket rope flashing between the pawing front legs before it crashed to the ground on top of the King, and rolled over him. I was one of the N.C.Os who helped to push the horse off and carry His Majesty to his car.*
>
> *Everyone was sworn to secrecy lest the Germans got news of the accident, and the Squadron was detailed to patrol over the hospital at Aire throughout the time the royal patient lay there.*

King George was not overly fond of the RAF, much preferring the traditions and impressive battleships of the Royal Navy, and it is unlikely this incident endeared the new service to him.

Return south west on the N41 and continue ahead over the junction with the D188. Turn left in the centre of Bruay at the traffic lights into an un-numbered road. There is a sign post with several arms, the bottom one of which is marked MAPAD "Edith Piaf". Continue ahead up the hill and after the first traffic lights the Stade-Parc Municipal Roger Salengers will appear on the right. Park in front of this.

Bruay Aerodrome

Much careful research was conducted on the location of this aerodrome, comparing trench maps with modern maps. Unfortunately, for such an historic spot, it has now largely disappeared beneath a park and sports track.

The first unit to arrive was 3 Squadron, on 15 March 1916, and at various times 16, 18, 23, 35, 46, 54 and 4 Australian Squadrons were based here. However, the airfield is synonymous with 40 Squadron, who occupied it from 29 April 1917 until 4 June 1918.

In *Airfields and Airmen, Ypres*, page 106 the career of the great British

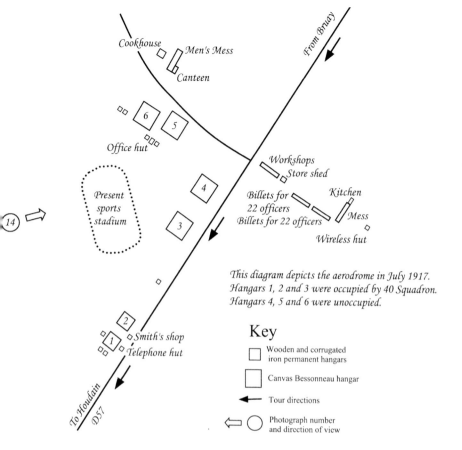

Cookhouse · Men's Mess
Canteen
From Bruay

6 · 5
Office hut

Present sports stadium

4

Workshops
Store shed

Billets for 22 officers · Kitchen
Billets for 22 officers · Mess
Wireless hut

3

14

This diagram depicts the aerodrome in July 1917.
Hangars 1, 2 and 3 were occupied by 40 Squadron.
Hangars 4, 5 and 6 were unoccupied.

Key

☐ Wooden and corrugated iron permanent hangars

☐ Canvas Bessonneau hangar

← Tour directions

⇦ ◯ Photograph number and direction of view

2
1 · Smith's shop
Telephone hut

To Houdain
D57

Picture No. 14: Bruay looking to the east in 2003

TRAFFIC LIGHTS

AERODROME

D57

Mannock seated in his Nieuport Scout at Bruay. The spinner on the propeller was a non-standard fitting.

ace, Mick Mannock was described. He arrived at 40 Squadron on 2 April 1917

40 Squadron

Formed at Gosport on 26 February 1916 from a nucleus of 23 Squadron, it arrived at St Omer on 19 August 1916. From August 1916 until April 1917 the unit operated from Treizennes and after only a few days at Auchel moved to Bruay. The initial equipment was the RAF FE8, a pusher, which was obsolescent by the time it arrived at the front. 40 Squadron was one of only two operational units to be fully equipped with

A standard RFC double Lewis gun ammunition drum. See *Ypres*, page 28 for more information. While stowed in the cockpit of a Nieuport it was hit by an enemy bullet, most probably saving the pilot from serious injury or death. The damage can be seen top right. The pilot, Gerry Crole, after service with 40 Squadron, was taken prisoner as a flight commander with 43 Squadron.

The bottom of a Nieuport inter wing strut showing the notorious bottom fitting responsible for a number of structural failures (*Somme*, page 182.) The item has been replaced as there is a bullet hole where the two sections meet. This unit was almost certainly fitted to Nieuport B1552 in which Mick Mannock claimed his second victory.

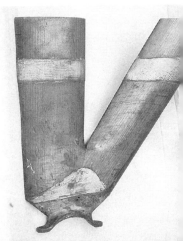

the type. On 12 March 1917 the first Nieuport Scout arrived and on the 22nd the last of the FE8s were returned to the aircraft depot.

Joachim von Bertrab *Jasta* 30

During his first month with 40 Squadron Mannock was involved in a number of inconclusive combats and it was not until 7 May 1917 he had his first decisive encounter, when he shot a kite balloon down in flames. He soon settled in and his victories mounted. On 22 July he was awarded the MC and promoted to captain, in command of a flight, having claimed four enemy machines. He was now able to implement his ideas on tactics and how a flight should be run.

In August 40 Squadron had a number of machines operating from an advanced landing ground at Mazingarbe, just south of Béthune. This was a small grass area just behind the lines, and was employed for strafing the enemy trenches and for quick sorties to catch enemy aeroplanes seen from or reported to the field. All the pilots were volunteers and Mannock was one of the regulars who performed this duty. On 12 August 1917 he flew an offensive patrol, taking off at 1440 hours. At 1510 hours he spotted a dark painted Albatros DIII. In his diary he wrote:

> *19 August 1917 (Sunday)*
>
> *Had a splendid fight with a single-seater Albatross Scout last week on our side of the lines and got him down. This proved to be Lieutenant von Bartrap (sic), Iron Cross, and had been flying for eighteen months. He came over for one of our balloons - near Neuville - St - Vaast - and I cut him off going back. He didn't get the balloon either. The scrap took place at two thousand feet up, well within view of the whole front. And the cheers! It took me five minutes to get him to go down, and I had to shoot him before he would land. I was very pleased I did not kill him. Right arm broken by a bullet, left arm and left leg deep flesh wounds. His machine, a beauty, just issued (1 June 1917) with a 220 h.p. Mercedes engine , all black with crosses picked out in white lines - turned over on landing and was damaged. Two machine guns with one thousand rounds of ammunition against my single Lewis and three hundred*

Joachin von Bertrab standing by his Albatros. It has been variously described as purple or black in colour. The comet design on the fuselage was his personal marking.

RE8 A3196 '14'of 16 Squadron at Bruay May 1917, showing their double white bar marking. This unit was based at Bruay from August 1916 until May 1917.

rounds! I went up to the trenches to salve 'bus' later, and had a great ovation from everyone. Even Generals congratulated me. He didn't hit me once.

At the conclusion of the scrap Mannock landed at the Mazingarbe advanced landing ground.

Von Bertrab had a meteoric start to his career. After service with *FA 71* he was posted to *Jasta* 30, based at Phalempin, south of Lille, on 6 March 1917 (see page 28). A month later, on 6 April, he made his first claim and shot down four machines in one day! He brought down two Martinsyde Elephants from 27 Squadron and two Sopwith 11/2 Strutters from 45 Squadron. Of the eight crew members, six were killed and two were taken prisoner. All the fatalities are buried in Tournai Communal Cemetery, Allied Extension (see page 54). *Oberleutnant* Hans Bethge, commanding the *jasta*, also brought down a 11/2 Strutter of 45 Squadron and these crews also are buried or commemorated at Tournai. Out of 45 Squadron's formation of eight machines, four were lost, just to take eleven photographs.

Having set off at a great pace, von Bertrab did not score again until 15 May, when he brought down an FE2 of 20 Squadron, whose crew were made prisoner. Again, Bertrab had a quiet patch and made no further claims until he was shot down by Mannock. He had been awarded both classes of the Iron Cross and spent the rest of the war as a prisoner.

40 Squadron converted to the SE5a in October but Mannock was to claim only one victory flying this type, before being posted home on 2 January 1918. While at Bruay he had claimed sixteen enemy machines, been awarded an MC and Bar and had become a seasoned fighter pilot.

Continue ahead on the D57 and at a roundabout turn right onto the D301. Turn right on the D341 to Calais and St Omer. At a roundabout go left to Chamblain Chatelain and Pernes. Proceed through Pernes and then turn right on an un-numbered road towards Heuchie. Just after leaving Pernes the cemetery is on the left.

Pernes British Cemetery

We are visiting the grave (II E38) of one of the great naval pilots of the First World War, Roderic Dallas, which is situated towards the middle of the cemetery on the right hand side.

The burial ground (14/24) was only begun in April 1918 when the 1st and 4th Canadian Casualty Clearing Stations were forced back here by the advancing German army. Later, three more CCSs were based here and nearly all the casualties are from these units. Unusually, of the total of over 1,000 commemorations or burials here, very few were brought in from the battlefields after the Armistice.

Roderic Stanley Dallas (II E38)

Our new CO, Dallas, is a splendid lad. Tall, good-looking, a wonderful specimen of manhood, very reserved and charming; a veritable flapper's idol! He hasn't flown much with us yet, but I think he will when he gets straightened out. He has a great score of Huns, varying from 30-37. He was considered the star turn of the RNAS and the practical expert adviser. So we were pretty lucky to get him.

The original Dallas grave marker at Pernes.

This was a description from a letter home by Captain Gwilym Lewis, a flight commander in 40 Squadron.

Dallas was born on 30 July 1891 at Mount Stanley, Queensland. Joining the Australian army in 1913 he volunteered for the RFC after the outbreak of war but was rejected. Fortunately, the RNAS accepted him and he began training in May 1915. He joined 1 Naval Wing at Dunkirk on 3 December 1915, flying both single and two-seaters on general work, such as reconnaissance and bombing. His first enemy machine was claimed on 22 April 1916 while flying a Nieuport. Most of his early victories were scored flying these machines, though two were gained on the Sopwith Triplane prototype. By the time part of 1 Wing had detached and become 1 Naval Squadron and equipped completely with the Triplane, Dallas had received a DSC and been made a flight commander.

Owing to the shortage of fighters in the RFC, 1 Naval was transferred to the Somme area in February 1917. April may have been Bloody April to the RFC but in that month Dallas claimed eight German aircraft. He was awarded a bar to his DSC and in June was given command of 1 Naval,

Roderic Dallas in his 40 Squadron SE5a D3511. He claimed five of his 32 victories in this machine.

which in the autumn converted to the legendary Sopwith Camel.

On 1 April 1918 the RAF was formed by the amalgamation of the RFC and RNAS. 40 Squadron had lost its commanding officer on 9 March when Major L A Tilney had been brought down and killed (see page 129) and Dallas was posted in as the new commander. In April and May he claimed another nine enemy machines, despite having been wounded.

Gwilym Lewis again:

The spirit of this squadron is simply wonderful now. All due to the 'Admiral' or the 'Old Fool' as we sometimes call him. Everyone adores him and everyone is full out to bring Huns down as a result.

On 1 June Dallas took off at 1010 hours on a solo Offensive Patrol in Camel No. D3530 and failed to return, as Gwilym Lewis described in a letter home:

The world is upside down. I don't know where to start. In the first place Dallas has been killed. I can't think why, but he has been. Too good for this world, I suppose. As was his custom, he went out on his own to strafe high reconnaissance machines. He must have been coming back when he saw a Triplane just our side of the Lines. Of course, it had to be destroyed, and in the meantime two other Triplanes descended from a great height, and shot the poor fellow through the head. He fell this side of the Lines, with a very sound 40 Huns to his credit. He never claimed anything he wasn't absolutely certain of.

We simply couldn't believe our ears when we first got the news, but all the same it was true. It wasn't a matter of admiring the 'old fool'; we simply adored him. He must have had a most wonderful influence because the squadron has had awfully bad luck, and a very large element of new pilots. Yet the spirit has been wonderful. There never was such a happy bunch of lads. I feel I have lost a very good friend as well as a CO. Since I returned from leave we got to know each other awfully well, and had all sorts of discussions on the squadron and pilots in it. He had got everyone summed up properly, and he knew everything worth knowing about the lads. He seldom,

Pilots of 40 Squadron at Bruay in April 1918. Roderick Dallas is third from the right and Gwilym Lewis fourth from the right.

if ever, said or seemed to think anything but nice things about everybody.

The worst of the whole thing was that he had almost fixed up to take charge of all testing in England, and we all saw possibilities of a sort of reunion in England under him. However, that is no more, and we no longer have our 'Admiral'.

Leutnant Johannes Werner

Dallas was officially credited to Johannes Werner of *Jasta* 14. Werner had claimed one Allied machine with an unknown unit prior to being given command of *Jasta* 14 on 5 September 1917, a position he held until the end of the war. On 1 June 1918 he had taken off from Phalempin (see page 28) where *Jasta* 14 were based, on a balloon raid. He attacked and shot down Dallas as his sixth and penultimate victory.

Johannes Werner (right) when an observer with *FA* 45 on the Eastern Front.

When he received a Fokker DVIII, his Fokker Triplane was taken over by *Gefreiter* Preiss, who became a prisoner of war on 9 June 1918, when he was brought down by SE5s of No. 1 Squadron RAF. Today (2003) the rudder from this machine is on display in the 1 Squadron crew room.

Return to Pernes and at the T junction turn right for Amiens and St Pol. Continue south on the D916 and then the N41 into St Pol. At the bottom of the long hill turn left round the fountain into Place de Marechal Leclerc. Proceed up the hill and take the first left turn to the Cimetière Est, then follow green War Graves Commission sign to St Pol Communal Cemetery Extension. The British plot is behind the French military graves.

St Pol Communal Cemetery Extension

The two casualties we have come to see, H F Hughes and J L M Sandy (H 8 and H10), were involved in one of the more bizarre episodes of the air war. They are in the furthest row from the entrance near the left hand end.

St Pol-sur-Ternoise was an administrative centre for the British army and No. 12 Stationary Hospital was established on the race course near the town in June 1916, and remained for three years. The Allied Extension (13/1) was attached to the very old *Cimetière Thuillier* and is in the corner of the French military cemetery.

No. 69 (Australian) Squadron

In *Airfields and Airmen, Cambrai,* page 103 the circumstances surrounding the capture of the Albatros DVa in the National Air and Space Museum, Washington were described. The only other original example of this type is in the Australian War Memorial, Canberra and its history is also very interesting

Unlike the other members of the British Empire, Australia formed its own separate squadrons during the war, although many Australians continued to serve with the RFC, RNAS and RAF.

69 (Australian) Squadron was formed on 28 December 1916 and after employing the usual assortment of aeroplanes, received their first RE8s in August 1917. Fully equipped with these machines they flew to St Omer on 9 September 1917 and then settled into their permanent base at Bailleul (*Ypres*, page 69) at the beginning of November. Their duties were standard corps work of reconnaissance, bombing and artillery ranging.

It was on one of these missions that Lieutenant James Lionel Montague Sandy and his observer, Sergeant Henry Francis Hughes departed on 17 December 1917. They left the Town Ground Aerodrome, Bailleul at 1415 hours to cooperate with the 8 inch howitzers of 151 Siege Battery. The shoot continued until 1452 hours when they were attacked by enemy aircraft. Another 69 Squadron crew, Lieutenant E H Jones and Lieutenant K C Hodgson became involved:

At about 2.55 p.m. we noticed five E.A. attacking RE8 No. A3816

RE8 A3662 'J' of 69 (Australian) Squadron at the Town Ground, Bailleul. This was a Presentation Machine, having been bought from funds provided by Mr H Teesdale Smith of Adelaide.

between DEULEMENT and ARMENTIERES. We went to his assistance and joined the combat. The observer fired 400 rounds and at 3.05 p.m. the EA withdrew. We flew round close to the other RE8 to see his number and found that it was No. A3816, Lieut. H. L. Sandy. He was then apparently all right and passed our machine flying North. We returned to the aerodrome for more ammunition and on reaching the line a second time did not see Lieut. Sandy anywhere.

Another report was received from 2nd Southern Anti-Aircraft Group:

At 2.55 p.m., 17.12.17, six enemy fighters came over our lines in the vicinity of ARMENTIERES and attacked an RE8 which was on duty near there. Although hard pressed by the E.A., the RE8 would not give up but put up a hard fight against his six opponents. Finally one of the Hun machines was seen to be hit and to come down in the direction of FRELINGHEIN. Two other RE8's came up and joined in the combat and the E.A. withdrew. One RE8 was seen to proceed homewards, the other two continued duty.

Confirmation of the downed enemy machine came from 2nd Division General Staff, who reported:

An enemy machine, Pilot slightly wounded, landed this afternoon at Sheet 36C8c.80.95.

This machine has been collected and the Pilot handed over to the Corps Cage.

The German Pilot states that he was brought down by a two-seater machine, a bullet having gone through his petrol tank.

By 1800 hours nothing had been heard from Sandy and Hughes. Eventually the machine, with their bodies still inside, was found over 50 miles away on the St Pol - Bruay road, having landed at 1500 hours. It was surmised that a single shot had killed both of them and the machine, being very stable, had circled for more than two hours, before making a soft landing after its fuel ran out.

Clauss' Albatros DVa, number 5390/17, at the factory before it was delivered to *Jasta* 29.

Sandy, the son of Mr. J M Sandy and Mrs E M Sandy of Burwood, New South Wales, had completed his training with 81 and 82 Squadrons in the spring of 1917. He had then spent two months serving with 53 Squadron in France, before arriving at 69 Squadron on 10 September. Hughes was the son of Terence and Henrietta Hughes of South Yarra, Victoria.

Such is the lack of German records that the christian name of the German pilot involved is unknown. *Leutnant* Clauss served in *Jasta* 29 from June 1917 but spent some time in *Kest* 1a, before hospitalisation. He claimed one victory, on 13 November 1917, for which there is no corresponding Allied loss. His aeroplane was allocated the captured number G101.

On 19 January 1918 69 Squadron was re-numbered No. 3 Squadron, Australian Flying Corps. They remained independent after the amalgamation of the RNAS and RFC to form the RAF.

Return to the centre of town and continue through St Pol. Turn left on the D916 to Amiens and then left again on the N39 to Arras. Exit the dual carriageway right on the D81 to Ligny-St-Flochel. Continue through the village towards Averdoingt and the cemetery is on the left.

Ligny-St-Flochel British Cemetery

The first grave, Captain LP Watkins (I E1), we are visiting is connected with the bombing of Great Britain by German airships and is situated at the end of the fifth row on the right side of the cemetery, adjacent to the seat.

This burial ground (14/31) was begun in April 1918 when the 7th Casualty Clearing Station was established here. Later three more CCS's were set up but all three had gone by November 1918. There are a total of 632 graves, plus 46 Germans in a separate extension on the right hand side.

The Zeppelin

It is difficult now to imagine the terror and panic wrought by the German airship raids over Britain in the Great War, given that over 50,000 civilians were killed during Second World War bombing, without morale collapsing or the outbreak of mass hysteria. Perhaps the population, after centuries of stable existence, secure in the knowledge that the Royal Navy would prevent any attacks on the country, suddenly found itself at the mercy of a foreign power. Another factor was that, initially, there seemed to be no effective defence against them.

After their unopposed bombing campaign in 1915, the Germans suffered considerable setbacks in 1916. The L30 Class of Zeppelin was introduced in May 1916 and had a ceiling of 13,000 feet. With improved

The Zeppelin L48.

defences, consisting of more anti-aircraft guns, more aeroplanes and searchlights, the British flying services had enough warning for their machines to climb to the airship's cruising height. Intelligence, gathered from the monitoring of enemy radio messages, gave further advanced warning. In 1916 four naval Zeppelins and one army Schütte-Lanz were shot down, of which four came down in flames, raising the morale of the British public.

The leader of the Naval Airship Division, *Korvettenkapitän* Peter Strasser, realised that they had to fly higher. Four L30 airships under construction were the subject of a thorough weight saving programme. The new L48, embodying all the modifications, was completed in May 1917. It had a ceiling of 20,000 feet, which Strasser hoped would enable him to recommence his bombing campaign. Unfortunately, the height at which it now flew brought its own problems. The crew suffered from lack of oxygen which caused altitude sickness, the engines were not as powerful due to the less dense atmosphere and the unpredictable winds over the North Sea were stronger at altitude.

Captain Loudon Pearce Watkins MC (I E1)

On the night of 16/17 June 1917 Strasser raided Britain with his 'Height Climbers'. The force consisted of the Zeppelins L42, L44, L45, L46, L47 and L48. Strasser's deputy, *Korvettenkapitän*, Victor Schutze elected to lead the force from his flagship, the L48. Problems beset the mission from the start, when two of the airships could not get out of their sheds due to cross winds and another two returned because of engine problems. The remaining pair continued and their presence alerted all the English east coast defences. The L48 was having problems with its engines and at one stage all motors were shut down and she drifted silently along, while repairs were carried out. A salvo of thirteen bombs was dropped in the Harwich area, without causing any casualties.

The airship reduced height to take advantage of a tailwind and then, at 0325 hours it was attacked by three British aeroplanes. Two machines had taken off from Orfordness. Though an experimental station the pilots were

The L48 after being shot down in flames. Note the ring of sentries around the wreck to prevent looting.

expected to respond to calls when there was hostile activity. One machine, an FE2b, was crewed by Lieutenant F D Holder and Sergeant Sydney Ashby. The second aeroplane was a DH2 flown by Robert Saundby, who had served in 24 Squadron with Lanoe Hawker VC and been part of the patrol when Hawker was killed (*Somme*, page 83). The third machine was a BE12 from 37 Squadron, a dedicated home defence unit, based at Goldhanger in Essex and was flown by L P Watkins.

The L48 was hit in two places and a flame appeared in the nose. This ran along the spine of the airship and was followed by an explosion. The airship became a mass of flame, as nearly 2,000,000 cubic feet of highly inflammable hydrogen ignited. She slowly sank to earth at a 60 degree tail down angle and after three long minutes crashed into a field at Theberton in Suffolk. The huge fireball was witnessed by the horrified crew of the L42 from 70 miles away. Amazingly, three crew members survived, though one died of his injuries on Armistice Day 1918. The crew were buried in

An FE2 of 148 Squadron prepares to depart.

A group of 148 Squadron aircrew. L P Watkins is in the centre.

Theberton churchyard, where the only wreath came from the officers at Orfordness. In 1966 the remains of the crew, together with the other three German airship crews brought down on British soil, were transferred to the German cemetery at Cannock Chase in Staffordshire.

It was difficult to establish which of the three RFC machines had delivered the mortal blow to the L48, so the sensible decision was made to award all three pilots the MC and Ashby the Military Medal.

Watkins, a Canadian, born on 26 March 1897, was a student at Upper Canada College, Toronto from 1911 to 1915. After arriving in the UK he trained at Castle Bromwich at the close of 1915 then joined 7 Squadron in France on 11 May 1916. Posted to 21 Squadron in July and then 34 Squadron in December, he returned to the UK, and was transferred to 37 Squadron, as a flight commander. In early 1918 he arrived at 148 Squadron, who were forming as a night bombing unit for service in France. On 25 April 1918 they landed at Auchel, west of Béthune.

Just after midnight, on the morning of 1 July 1918, Watkins and his observer, Lieutenant Charles William Wridgway, left on their second bombing sortie of the night, loaded with one 112 lb bomb and two 20 lb bombs. About 45 minutes after departure they had engine failure, when No. 3 cylinder rocker arm broke. During the subsequent forced landing in standing corn, the machine over-turned, throwing Wridgway out and injuring him. Watkins died as the result of a broken neck - a sad end after so much operational flying.

Wridgway, who was born in Bexhill on 14 June 1898, had been educated at Manchester Grammar School. After a few months apprenticeship with the Darracq motor company, he was successful in the Army Entrance Exam and went to the Royal Military College, Sandhurst. Commissioned into the Middlesex Regiment, he joined the RFC in

October 1917. After recovering from his injuries received on the night of 1 July 1918, he was demobilised on 19 September 1919. For many years he worked in the test department of Crossley Motors and then became an industrial consultant. He died in 1961.

Hans Reimers *Jasta* 6

The next grave (E 8) we are visiting is in the very back row of the German plot on the right hand side of the cemetery. This casualty illustrates the problem historians face when official records are poor or even non-existent. With the loss of the German air service records during the Second World War, we are reliant on surviving notes made by diligent German enthusiasts in the 1930s. The *Jasta* 6 diary only shows Reimers as having left on a patrol and failing to return. He was born on 29 October 1894 in Hamburg, and joined *Jasta* 6 on 21 July 1918. On 8 August he claimed a French Breguet bomber and the following day a DH 9. Wounded on 4 September, he died the following day.

Hans Reimers in Fokker EV 152/18.

It is almost certain that his victor was Captain Arthur Treloar Whealy of 203 Squadron. Born on 2 November 1893, Whealy, a Canadian, joined the RNAS in Canada and was commissioned in February 1916. Joining No. 3 Wing in June he was then posted to C Flight of 3 Naval, who were flying Sopwith Pups. His first victory was scored on 12 April 1917 when he sent an Albatros DIII down out of control. He then served for a short time in 9 Naval where he claimed four German machines and also flew the Sopwith Triplane. In November he rejoined 3 Naval, who had by now been re-equipped with the Sopwith Camel. Between February and September he claimed a total of nineteen victories and was awarded the DSC and bar

Three pilots of 3 (Naval) Squadron. Whealy is in the middle.

plus a DFC. On 4 September 1918, while on an offensive patrol with his flight, he saw a British kite balloon going down in flames. Observing a Fokker DVII he pursued it and fired 150 rounds at 100 yards range. It went down and crashed just east of Havrincourt Wood, southwest of Cambrai. This was most likely Reimers and was Whealy's twenty-seventh and last claim. Three weeks later he left 203 Squadron at the end of his tour of duty and returned to the UK.

Return to the N39 and continue towards Arras. Go straight ahead past the D62 left turn to Acq. Take the next unmarked left turn through Ecoivres on the D49. Cross the D341 and stop at the first crossroad. The aerodrome is ahead on the right hand side.

Mont-St-Éloi Aerodrome

This aerodrome is unusual in that only units of the Royal Naval Air Service were based here. The remains of the ruined abbey on the hill are a

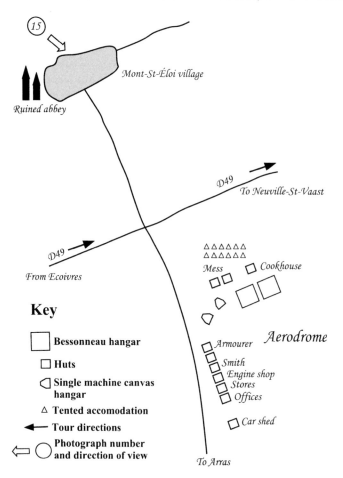

Picture No. 15: Mont-St-Éloi looking southeast.

very distinctive landmark.

No. 3 Naval Squadron inhabited Mont-St-Éloi for a very short time in March 1918 but the main resident unit was 8 Naval, who occupied it from May 1917 until February 1918. Many of the top naval aces flew from this spot, such as R A Little (see page 166), C D Booker (*Somme*, page 66), R R Soar, Chris Draper, Harold Day, S J Goble, J B White, G W Price, W L Jordan and E G Johnstone,

Geoffrey Bromet, the commander of 8 Naval, later wrote:

> *The squadron moved up to St. Eloi on May 16th and quickly settled down under most comfortable conditions. The machines were moved in to two Bessoneau hangars and all the personnel were*

*under canvas except for Messes, offices, etc. The aerodrome was
large with a splendid surface and excellent approaches, and was
ideally situated for the nature of our work. We were 14500 yards
from Oppy and 11000 yards from Lieven, and although some people
thought we might be too near the lines for safety I never entertained
that idea and was very pleased with our position.*

Bromet (later Air Vice-Marshal Sir Geoffrey Bromet KBE, CB, DSO) was
an extremely able squadron commander, and much respected. E D
Crundall, an ace with 8 Naval, had this to say of him in his book *Fighter
Pilot on the Western Front*:

> *When I went into the Officers Mess Thornley was sitting there by
> himself. He told me he had just returned from a walk to Mont St Eloi
> village with Squadron Commander Bromet. The CO took him to a
> place on the hill from where they could look down on the aerodrome
> and get a bird's eye view of the whole squadron. The CO told
> Thornley he is very proud of his squadron and thinks a lot of all who
> serve under him. Thornley told him that all of us have the greatest
> admiration for him and look upon him as the father of the squadron.
> Thornley told me he often goes for walks with Squadron
> Commander Bromet who likes to have his company because he is
> ❧lder than the rest of us. Thornley is twenty-eight years of age, the
> old man of the squadron so far as the pilots are concerned, and
> Squadron Commander Bromet is twenty-five.*

E D Crundall, again, on how the pilots spent their spare time:

> *19 July*
>
> *As there is no flying this morning the pilots are amusing
> themselves in various ways. Johnson is flying a model aeroplane,
> which he built, and it goes quite a long way. Little made a submarine
> out of a piece of wood, to which he fitted metal fins. It is propelled
> by elastic and he is demonstrating it in the swimming pool. The*

The Camels of 208 Squadron at Mont-St-Éloi.

swimming pool was dug by the pilots and has a wooden framework around its sides to which balloon fabric is attached. This makes the pool watertight and prevents dirt from getting into it.

24 July

In the afternoon some of us were in the swimming pool when we heard a machine gun. We saw an Albatros scout attack the Kite Balloon near our aerodrome boundary. The Kite Balloon went down in flames. Two pilots got into their Triplanes, quite naked except for boots, but could not catch the Albatros.

From the hill adjacent to the ruined abbey there is a good view down on to the aerodrome. Chris Draper, the so-called 'Mad Major' (*Ypres*, page 95), is reputed to have flown between the two columns of the ruin. It looks possible but I have to say it must have taken incredible nerve and skill.

Continue ahead on the D49 and then turn left on the D937 to Béthune. Proceed ahead and the cemetery is on the left.

Cabaret Rouge British Cemetery

Many of the Commonwealth War Graves Commission cemeteries have unusual names and this is one of my favourites. The name derived from a house on the main road, about one kilometre south of Souchez village.

The cemetery (15/77) is very large and contains the remains of more than 7,600 British and Commonwealth forces of whom, sadly, over half are unidentified. It was begun in March 1916 and used until August 1917 and at various periods until September 1918. After the Armistice over 7,000 casualties were brought here from the battlefields and 103 other burial grounds. In May 2000 a Canadian unknown soldier was exhumed from here, taken to Ottowa and interred in the Tomb of the Unknown Warrior at the National War Memorial. The new headstone (VIII E7), situated to the left of the Stone of Remembrance, describes this.

There are 79 flying casualties, including ten from 43 Squadron and twelve from 25 Squadron, both of which were based at nearby Lozinghem.

Egg on my face (XV G22, 23 and 24)

For many years now there has been an annual British Airways tour of the Western Front. We call ourselves the Heathrow Pals, and I am the so-called 'expert' on First War flying. One of the most frequently asked questions I have had to answer is why RFC casualties have the RAF badge on the headstone, despite the fact this organisation was only established on 1 April 1918. The first time the party visited Cabaret Rouge the question was asked again. I replied by saying I did not know, as I had never seen one and then rashly stated that "you will never find an RFC badge". It is always dangerous making sweeping statements, for a voice behind me said "What, like this one?" and then another voice, "And this one?" There are a number of RFC headstones in this cemetery but, on the whole, they are not that common and there is no rhyme or reason to their use. The Royal Navy, being different of course, uses the fouled anchor for RNAS casualties.

By a curious chance, and you almost feel it may have been deliberate, in Plot XV, row G, which is half left from the Stone of Remembrance, there are examples of all three designs alongside each other. There is an unknown officer with an RAF badge, Second Lieutenant P C Wood with an RFC emblem, and Flight-Sub-Lieutenant H A Pailthorpe with the fouled anchor of the RNAS.

In a letter to the noted aviation author Norman Franks some years ago, the great naval ace, Ray Collishaw, who claimed 60 victories, explained his views on headstone badges of the RNAS units attached to the RFC:

As the Naval Fighter Squadrons were under RFC operational control and they were called upon to do exactly the same as RFC squadrons, they were to all intents and purposes RFC squadrons. There is a curiosity about this - while all RFC and RAF grave headstones bear large 'wings' upon them, RNAS headstones bear only a 'fouled anchor' and no 'wings'. The 'fouled anchor' was never the symbol of the RNAS and the use of this symbol, in my opinion, is especially inappropriate on RNAS graves of airmen killed while working with the army.

Leonard Arthur Tilney (XV Q37)

The next grave we have come to see is in the second row from the back of Plot XV, which is half left from the Stone of Remembrance.

Tilney, born on 7 June 1895, served in the Duke of Lancaster's Yeomanry and then obtained a commission in the Royal Horse Guards. In

January 1915 he joined the RFC at South Farnborough and after CFS was posted to 11 Squadron at Netheravon in Wiltshire. In late July the squadron joined the British Expeditionary Force and established themselves at Vert Galand (*Somme*, page 45). On 29 August 1915, Tilney had an operation for appendicitis and was in hospital at Rouen until late September. Promoted to flight commander in December and after training appointments at home, he was sent to France to command 40 Squadron, on 7 February 1917.

Harold Balfour (later Lord Balfour of Inchrye) had this to say of him in his book, *An Airman Marches:*

Leonard Tilney.

Nieuport Scout B1617. After service in 29 Squadron it flew with 40 Squadron. Major Tilney returned it to No. 1 Aircraft Depot on 14 October 1917. It was later held on charge of 60 Squadron as the personal aircraft of Brigadier-General J H W Becke, commanding II Brigade.

It was about this time that Robert Loraine was succeeded by Leonard Tilney, who was one of the finest "pusher" pilots of the day. Leonard Tilney had left Eton just before the War, and was still only a boy in years, looking about nineteen, with his fair hair and ruddy complexion. Nevertheless, he took over No. 40 Squadron, and proved one of the best young Squadron Commanders that the Flying Corps has ever produced.

On 9 March 1918, Tilney was part of a twelve-man Offensive Patrol in the Douai area. At 1600 hours they dived on a German formation and three were claimed out of control. Unfortunately, Tilney failed to return and it was believed that his aircraft broke up in the air. Another pilot, P La T Foster, also failed to return and was made prisoner, due to engine failure. In addition Captain R J Tipton was wounded.

Sergt. A.G.Adams, M.T. A.S.C. ,attached 'C' Bty A.A. states:-

At about 4-45 pm on 9/3/18 I saw an SE5 coming in very low from direction of LENS. He circled over CALONNE ROAD and made a good landing behind our billet. (R.11.b.2.7.)

I received orders to mount a guard and take charge of the machine.

I found Capt. Tinton (Tipton), the pilot, was badly hit in the abdomen but was conscious. He gave me the number of his Squadron and said he didn't mind too much, because he got the Hun who hit him, and was quite cheerful owing to that fact.

I did not question him as he appeared to be very weak.

Tipton was admitted to No. 1 CCS but died three days later and is buried in Barlin Communal Cemetery Extension, southeast of Bruay.

Tilney was claimed by the very successful German ace Paul Billik.

Leutnant Paul Billik

Billik was born on 27 March 1881 and joined the German air service in May 1916. Posted to *Jasta* 12 in March 1917, he was awarded the Iron Cross First Class after his fourth victory. His first victim had been the noted ace, J J Malone DSC, of 3 Naval. In July 1917 he went to *Jasta* 7 and after his eighth victory, was posted to *Jasta* 52 as commanding officer. His first claim in this unit was the unfortunate Tilney. Billik's number of victories mounted steadily and with a total of twenty-seven he was awarded the Knight's Cross with Swords of the Hohenzollern House Order and must surely have known the *Pour le Mérite* was not far off. However, on 10 August 1918, he landed in Allied lines and was made prisoner after his engine had been shot through. Though nominated for the Blue Max, with 31 victories, it was not awarded to Billik. Released in 1919, he was killed in a flying accident in Berlin on 8 March 1926.

Leutnant **Paul Billik, commanding** *Jasta* **52.**

Billik's Albatros with his personal marking. The swastika was considered a good luck symbol until it acquired more sinister associations.

Harry Alexander Taylor Kennedy (XV R23)

The last grave we are visiting is situated in the row behind Tilney and to the left.

I think this casualty is particularly sad as the victim was convinced he was not going to survive and yet forced himself to continue flying.

Kennedy, a Canadian who was born in November 1895, joined the RFC in late 1916, after a gruelling time in the trenches. He had spent ten months as a machine gun officer and in September had been wounded in the forehead by a shrapnel burst at Pozières. After initial training at Oxford, then 24 Reserve Squadron and the Central Flying School, he was posted to 40 Squadron at Bruay on 3 May 1917. Though he only claimed one enemy machine, on 15 August, he was a useful member of the squadron and well-liked. The squadron did not suffer the terrible casualties that the other RFC Nieuport equipped squadrons did, possibly due to flight commanders of the quality of Mick Mannock.

William MacLanachan, nicknamed McScotch by Mannock to differentiate him from George McElroy, who was McIrish, wrote of his time in the squadron in his excellent book, *Fighter Pilot:*

> We had discovered a teashop in a side street near the Officers' Club, a clean, fresh place owned by a dark, very attractive French girl, where we could obtain all the delicacies for which the country is famous. Mademoiselle admired 'Les Officiers Anglais' and, judging by the very reasonable prices she charged, her work must have been more of self-imposed duty than a profit-making business. We nicknamed her the 'Queen of Sheba'.
>
> Because of his knowledge of French, she and Kennedy were soon fast friends and their innocent flirtations over the teacups caused Mick and myself a great deal of amusement.

On the evening of 21 August, MacLanachan and Kennedy were based on the advanced landing ground at Mazingarbe, in anticipation of a very early patrol. MacScotch related a conversation between the two of them:

> Our mechanics warned us that we had better retire to bed as we had to be up so early, but Kennedy was restless and had no desire to sleep. He opened the portable gramophone and put on a record of a song which evidently appealed to him, for he played it over several times, humming the refrain and insisting that I should memorise the words . . .

> *I shall see you to-night, Love,*
> *In our beautiful dreamland,*
> *And your eyes will be bright, Dear,*
> *With the love-light that gleams for me.*
> *To my heart I will press you,*

I will kiss and caress you,
So good-night and God bless you,
I shall see you to-night.

I have neither heard nor seen the words of the song since, but so vivid is my memory of that night that I have written them down just as Kennedy sang them.

At last he put the record away, and a 'monitory' snore from the mechanics' tent reminded us that our fitters and riggers had to be up very early to prepare the machines for the patrol. Kennedy was silent for a few minutes, thoughtfully puffing his cigarette and sipping his drink. The stillness of the night was broken by spasmodic bursts of artillery fire - the Germans shelling Bully-Grenay, and the answering roar of our own twelve-inch howitzer. Until we could get accustomed to the noise sleep was impossible.

During a lull Kennedy turned to me: "Do you believe in hunches, Mac?"

I did not understand what he meant by 'hunch' until he explained that it was American slang for a premonition.

"I've got a powerful hunch," he said, "I shall never see my girl again - I'll never last out another day." Then he told me of his university life in Toronto, of his home life and of his fiancée. In conclusion he added: "And in another twenty-four hours, Mac, it'll be all over. What was the use of it?"

Kennedy was my age - twenty-one, and it was strange to hear him talking in this despondent way. I hated this talk of 'finishing'.

I told him the depressing effect of the shelling and the sentimental reminder of the song had encouraged his morbid thoughts, and advised him to try to sleep.

To my relief the next morning I saw him returning safe from the first patrol.

Later that day, after having completed a number of tiring patrols, they were taking their first drink and winding down for dinner:

We were helping ourselves when Major Tilney hurried into the mess.

"Blast them! he burst out. "Some fool of an observer has reported that Dorignies aerodrome is deserted, and we've got to corroborate the report tonight."

As a C.O. Major Tilney was considerate. We were tired.

He looked round the mess, and continued: "It's a dirty job - as if it matters whether we find out to-night or tomorrow morning. I've tried to put it off, but they say they must know before dark - looks like a job for you, Mac. You know those aerodromes round Douai."

On his own, MacScotch had little hope of making it back, as there were a number of very active enemy aerodromes in the area. After a discussion, largely led by Mick Mannock, it was agreed that two flights would provide high cover for MacLanachan. Flying at only ten or twenty feet he crossed the lines, found Dorignies and flew round it at low altitude. There was no sign of activity, so he climbed towards his escort. As he reached 5,000 feet, Mannock's flight dived on an enemy formation that Mac had observed earlier approaching from the northwest and were now directly above him. Within seconds there was a dogfight, with machines twisting and turning.

Zooming quickly as I let down my double Lewis gun in order to fire up into any German that got above me, I had almost gained their level when, to my horror, I saw a Nieuport careering downwards in a mad dive, streaks of smoke issuing behind it, while the sun vividly lit up the aluminium-painted fuselage and red, white and blue circles.

MacLanachan returned safely to Bruay and was met by Mannock:

When my machine stopped on the ground Mick ran out.

"Thank God you're safe, old boy! I thought you had gone too."

I asked him who were missing.

"Only Ken," he said mournfully, "I saw him going down."

We were able to claim several 'victories', but to Mick and myself these counted as nothing - we had lost Ken.

Ken had been very popular with the mechanics, and the next morning his fitter, Gilbert, almost tearful at the loss of 'his pilot', asked me if there were any chance of his being allowed to qualify as a pilot or even as an observer so that he could avenge his death. "They needn't give me any stripes, as long as they let me fight," he pleaded.

Such was the feeling of the majority of the mechanics for the fighting pilots; but Gilbert was too old, and good fitters were scarce.

Three days later Mick and I had an opportunity of taking tea at 'The Queen of Sheba's'. On entering the room I was acutely conscious of an air of depression and tension.

Mademoiselle took our order with a polite 'Oui, monsieur', and on her departure to make the tea Mick remarked on her apparent indifference to the absence of Kennedy.

As she was laying the cakes on the table he asked her; "Don't you wonder where our - your young friend is, mademoiselle?"

She nodded. "Certainement, monsieur le Capitaine, but I dare not ask. It is forbidden for us to ask any questions of the English officers. - Where is the nice English boy?" She looked round anxiously as if afraid of being overheard.

She could not speak English, so Mannock answered in the only word he knew to break it gently tp her.

"Il est parti," he said.

"Parti?" She was surprised and dubiously relieved.

"Parti -où?"

"Not that parti," Mick replied.*"Parti pour toujours- il est mort."*

'The Queen of Sheba', holding her dainty apron up to her mouth to suppress her sobs, hurried out of the room.

Poor mademoiselle - brave French girl, I am afraid many such episodes must have been the price of her devotion to her friendly work.

It is almost certain that Kennedy fell foul of Rudolf Wendelmuth of *Jasta* 8.

Rudolf Wendelmuth, *Jastas* 8 and 20.

Leutnant **Rudolf Wendelmuth**

Wendelmuth was born on 28 July 1890 in Gotha. After service in the 233rd Reserve Infantry Regiment, he transferred to the air service in March 1915. Following a period on the Bulgarian front and service in Cologne in a Fokker unit, he was then posted to Turkey. His first victory was scored here before he returned to the Western Front in April 1917, where he was posted to *Jasta* 8. His fifth victory, on 22 August 1917, was Kennedy. Having claimed eleven victories, he was posted to *Jasta* 20 as commanding officer in October 1917. Only three claims were made in this unit before he was killed in a mid-air collision with a machine from *Jasta* 4. He had been awarded both classes of the Iron Cross for his fourteen victories.

This concludes the second tour. Continue into Arras on the D937.

135

The Western Area

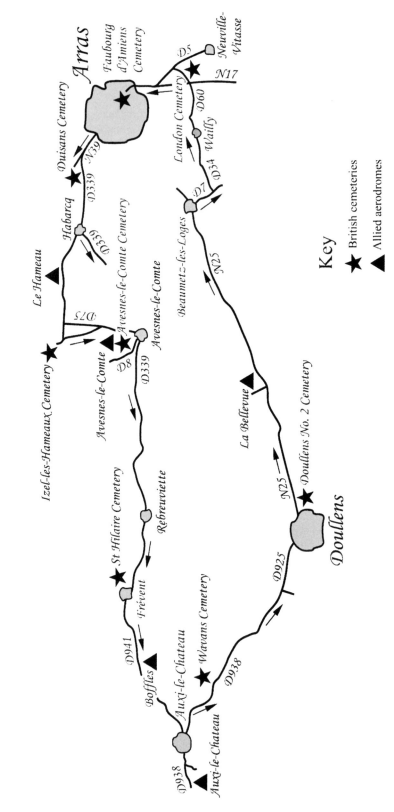

Key

★ British cemeteries

▲ Allied aerodromes

➤ Tour directions

Chapter Three

ARRAS: WESTERN AREA

This chapter covers an area which was far behind the British lines throughout the war, even after the German offensive of March 1918. The places that will be visited, together with the principal points of interest are:

Duisans British Cemetery - G R Howard, Commanding Officer 18 Squadron
Le Hameau Aerodrome - Billy Bishop VC
Izel-les-Hameaux Communal Cemetery - R L M Ferrie, 46 Squadron
Avesnes-le-Comte Communal Cemetery Extension - Major W A Grattan-Bellew
Avesnes-le-Comte Aerodrome - 12 Squadron
St Hilaire Cemetery Extension - Sergeant S J Mitchell AFM
Auxi-le-Chateau Aerodrome - McCudden VC crash site
Wavans British Cemetery - McCudden VC and R A Little
Doullens Communal Cemetery Extension No.2 - Mond and Martyn,
La Bellevue Aerodrome - 48 Squadron and Leefe Robinson VC
London Cemetery, Neuville-Vitasse - Stephen Dendrino 27 Squadron
Faubourg d'Amiens Cemetery - Paul Vogel *Jasta* 32b and the RAF Memorial

Leave Arras northwest on the N39 towards St Pol and turn left on the D339 to Avesnes-le-Comte and Frévent. Duisans British Cemetery will appear on the right.

Duisans British Cemetery

The first burials here were in February 1917, when the site was chosen for No. 8 Casualty Clearing Station. Most of the graves relate to the Battle of Arras and the subsequent trench warfare. There are a total of 3,205 British and Commonwealth casualties commemorated in the cemetery (14/37) plus 88 Germans.

I think this casualty is one of the most poignant, in that it was so close to the end of the war and was due to a silly accident. The cemetery is a most unusual shape, being a delta form, narrowing as the visitor approaches the Stone of Remembrance at the far end. The grave (VIII B24) we are visiting is located in the very last row, to the far right of the cemetery.

Guy Robert Howard (VIII B24)

Howard was born on 5 February 1886, his father was a colonel in the Royal Sussex Regiment. He was first commissioned into the militia during March 1903, and from September 1909 worked for the East Indian Railways. As a lieutenant, in the Essex Regiment, he earned one of the earliest DSOs of the First World War. The citation read:

> *While in command of a Patrol of the 2nd Battalion, Essex Regiment, on the 24th of September, to the south of Vregny, he made a valuable reconnaissance through a thick wood reaching a point 150 yards from the enemy's trenches.*

Major G R Howard.

Howard was also Mentioned in Despatches in November 1914.

In July 1915 he started his RFC training at Shoreham and, after CFS, joined 22 Squadron, crossing with them to France on 1 April 1916. They were equipped with FE2bs. At the beginning of August he was promoted to flight commander. Returning to Home Establishment, promotion to temporary major followed in January 1917 and on 20 November he was posted to command 18 Squadron at Auchel, west of Béthune. They had also been an FE2 unit, but in June of 1917 had re-equipped with the De Havilland DH4, a much superior machine altogether. The squadron changed aerodromes a number of times over the next year and on 13 October 1918 arrived at Le Hameau (see page 140).

On 23 October there was a party, described by Tich Rochford, a notable character and ace in 203 Squadron, in his book, *I Chose the Sky:*

> About the middle of October an example occurred of the excessive high spirits which from time to time broke out in our squadrons. Unfortunately, in this particular case it ended in tragedy. On the evening in question one of the squadrons at Izel-le-Hameau were having a party when some of its members decided to raid the mess of another squadron. Armed with Very light pistols one or two climbed on to the roof and fired them down the chimney. This started off a 'battle' between the two squadrons and very soon Very lights were being fired into the air in all directions, some of them landing on roofs of the hangars. Some of the more sober fellows on the aerodrome climbed up and kicked these off before

DH4 A7818 of 18 Squadron, crashed into a hut on 20 April 1918.

*they could start a fire. It was like a gigantic Guy Fawkes Night
celebration and those concerned seemed to be enjoying it a lot until
someone, firing a Very pistol at random, hit the CO of another
squadron behind an ear, severely injuring him. He was taken to
hospital where he died during the night. It was a tragic ending to a
very wild evening.*

For Howard it was a terrible way to end, having had a long war, in which
he had survived trench warfare and two operational tours with the RFC
and RAF. The Armistice celebrations in 18 Squadron, three weeks later,
were reported to have been rather muted!

A night victory

The next two graves we shall be visiting, Kurt Bratke and Hans
Heinrich (III O13 and O14) of *Bogohl* 3, are situated on the left side at the
back of Plot III.

Night bombing of the British rear areas had become a real problem in
1918 and to counter this, in June 1918, the RAF formed its first dedicated
night fighter squadron, No. 151, for service in France (*Cambrai*, page
145). On the night of 24/25 August 1918, they had ten machines patrolling
the Third Army area, including the commanding officer Major C J Q
Brand (*Ypres*, page 112). Just after midnight Lieutenant C R W Knight
shot a twin-engined machine down in flames, which crashed and blew up
east of Arras.

Two hours earlier, Lieutenant F C Broome and Captain D V Armstrong
encountered a Gotha type machine, which Broome noted in his combat
report had the letters FST on the fuselage:

*At 10.20 p.m. I observed E.A. from 9,000 ft. E.A. at 7,000 ft
approx. amid searchlights over No. 5 Lighthouse. I dived on to E.A.'s
tail and my engine cut out from pressure. I switched on gravity and
got under E.A.'s tail and fired a burst of 20 rounds E.A. replied. E.A.
was dodging in searchlights and I again got under tail and while
firing another 20 rounds got in E.A.'s backwash and spun. Another
Camel then engaged, fired and drew away. I closed with E.A. for the
third time and fired a long burst of 60 rounds, E.A. replying. I saw*

**A Gotha GVb. The main variants were the GIV and GV but the GVb was
introduced in limited numbers in 1918. Its distinguishing features were
extra wheels on the undercarriage to prevent nosing over during night
landings and a compound tail.**

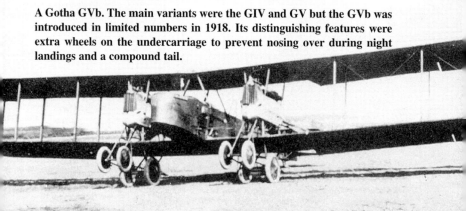

tracer going through fuselage and E.A. spun to 3,000 ft. approx., when I lost E.A. still spinning. I returned with machine and engine badly hit.

The machine, a Gotha Vb, was found crashed by 209 Squadron near to the No. 5 Lighthouse. Two of the crew, *Leutnant* Kurt Bratke and *Vizefeldwebel* Hans Heinrich were killed. The third member, who was taken prisoner, was probably *Vizefeldwebel* Lehmann. They belonged to *Bombenstaffel (Bosta)* 15, which was part of *Bombengeschwader (Boghol)* 3.

Frank Crossley Broome

'Tommy' Broome was born on 7 March 1892 and had been a mechanical engineer in Ashby de la Zouch before joining up. He volunteered for the RFC in September 1917. Joining 75 (HD) Squadron in October, he was then was posted to No. 112, another home defence unit. He went with his flight from this squadron when it was detached to form part of 151 Squadron. Before war's end he shot down two more enemy machines, including a giant Staaken (*Somme*, page 150). Broome returned to the UK in January 1919 and was demobilised two months later.

Tommy Broome later became a test pilot and then sales manager for the Vickers aircraft company.

Continue west along the D339 through Habarcq and Noyellette then turn right at a sign to Hermaville. At a crossroads turn left and continue past Filescamp Farm on your right and stop where the trees finish. The area on your right was the aerodrome.

Le Hameau Aerodrome

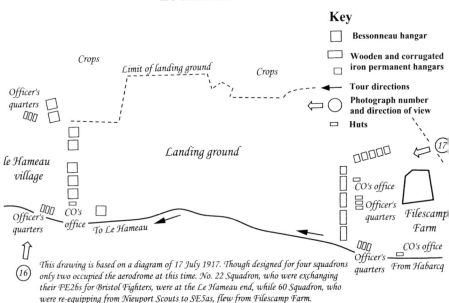

This drawing is based on a diagram of 17 July 1917. Though designed for four squadrons only two occupied the aerodrome at this time. No. 22 Squadron, who were exchanging their FE2bs for Bristol Fighters, were at the Le Hameau end, while 60 Squadron, who were re-equipping from Nieuport Scouts to SE5as, flew from Filescamp Farm.

Picture No. 16: A view looking north during the First World War of the Le Hameau or western end of the aerodrome.

Picture No. 17: View taken in 2001, looking west.

This was actually two aerodromes at the opposite ends of a very large field. The eastern end, which housed fighter squadrons, was based on Filescamp Farm, and the western end, housing two-seater units, backed on to the village of Le Hameau. It is often inaccurately referred to as Izel-les-Hameaux but this is another village about one kilometre further west. The squadrons that operated from here include: 1, 5, 11, 13, 18, 22, 23, 29, 32, 45, 52, 58, 59, 60, 64, 84, 94, 100, 101, 102, 203 and 209.

Of the two fields, Filescamp Farm has had the most publicity over the years because of the glamour attached to the fighter pilots who flew from here. Many of the top RFC and RAF aces were based on it at one time or another. Jimmy McCudden VC flew as a sergeant pilot with 29 Squadron and Albert Ball VC scored some of his victories while here with 60 Squadron.

Billy Bishop VC

Filescamp Farm is, perhaps, synonymous with Billy Bishop who, while flying here with 60 Squadron, claimed all his Nieuport Scout victories.

Bishop was born on 8 February 1894 in Owen Sound, Ontario and entered the Canadian Royal Military College in August 1911. He was regarded as the worst cadet the RMC had ever had and on the outbreak of war was awaiting the result of disciplinary proceedings. Fortunately for him there was such a shortage of officers that he was commissioned into the Mississauga Horse.

Bishop arrived in the UK in June 1915 but, soon tiring of the inactivity, applied to the RFC in July. After serving as an observer with 21 Squadron in France, he began pilot training during October 1916. In March 1917 he was posted to 60 Squadron at Filescamp Farm.

Never very good at landing aeroplanes, Bishop narrowly escaped being sent back to England after crashing a Nieuport. However, on 25 March he claimed his first victory, though two men in his patrol went missing. From this poor start he never looked back, with his second victory coming on 31 March. In April he claimed twelve enemy machines. In addition to when he was not flying on patrols he would go off on his own and many of his claims went uncorroborated, as there were no witnesses.

In April he was awarded an MC and received promotion to captain,

Nieuport B306 in which Bishop claimed his first victory on 25 March 1917. It is shown in use with a training unit in Egypt during 1918.

Billy Bishop in front of B1566. This was the highest scoring Nieuport Scout in the RFC.

followed shortly by a DSO.

On 2 June 1917, after a solo very early morning sortie to attack a German aerodrome, he returned with his machine shot about, claiming he had shot down three aircraft which had taken off to intercept him. For this feat Bishop, in an unprecedented case, received the Victoria Cross. In recent years there has been considerable and heated debate over this award and the veracity of Bishop's statement. However, regardless of any other consideration, it is an undeniable fact that the circumstances failed to meet the criteria laid down in the warrant governing the VC, as there were no witnesses and its award was entirely based on Bishop's account.

On 20 July 1917 Bishop claimed his last Nieuport victory, his 36th, most of them while flying B1566. No.60 Squadron started re-equipping with the SE5 in July and Bishop quickly appreciated the virtues of the new type. He scored eleven victories flying the SE and in August was posted to the UK, having also received a bar to his DSO.

During his time at Le Hameau, he claimed 47 victories and was the top RFC ace when he left France. Returning as commanding officer of 85 Squadron in 1918, he claimed a further 25 victories and received a DFC. At the end of the war he was the highest scoring British and Commonwealth ace with 72 claims. After the war he went into partnership with another Canadian ace and recipient of the VC, Billy Barker, in the flying business. In the Second World War he served again, as an Air Vice-Marshal, and died in Florida in 1953, at a comparatively early age.

Sholto Douglas had this to say of him:

I knew Bishop fairly well, and from time to time I came to see quite a lot of him; but there was something about him that left one feeling that he preferred to live as he fought: in a rather brittle, hard world of his own. He has been described as a lone wolf, but I do not think that any of us came to know him or to understand his motives well enough to be able to be sure about that. He was certainly not a lone wolf in the sense that we applied that description to Albert Ball.

With the passing of the years Billy Bishop mellowed in a noticeable way, and when I met him again in the Second World War - he was then an Air Marshal in the Royal Canadian Air Force - he seemed to have become more likeable and companionable.

Continue along the lane to just before the power lines. The other end of the aerodrome was by the trees on your right. Again proceed ahead until the crossroads at the end of the lane. Go straight over into the Chemin de l'Hopital. At the next crossroads turn right by the water tower on the D75E to Izel-les-Hameaux then left on the D54 in the village. Continue through the village and the cemetery is on the right.

Izel-les-Hameaux Communal Cemetery

There are only five flyers' graves in this civilian cemetery and they are on the left as you enter. Four of them served with 46 Squadron, who were based at Filescamp Farm at the time.

The first demonstrates how, in pre-antibiotics and penicillin days, even a minor wound could be fatal.

Eric Armitage

On 30 September 1917 C Flight of 46 Squadron, during an afternoon patrol, fell into a trap over Douai. While diving on two DFW two-seaters, they were in turn pounced on by five Albatros DVs. A mad dogfight commenced and the four Sopwith Pups were able to hold their own and did not have any casualties. After the sky had cleared they continued their patrol.

In his marvellous book *No Parachute*, Arthur Gould Lee wrote:

Within minutes we found two more D.F.W. two-seaters. The first at once turned east, and, forgetting Nobby's new tactics, we all dived on the second. As it dived away steeply, the observer fired at me and Armitage, who were nearest, but after about twenty shots I ran out of ammo. As I was pulling level, I saw Armitage, on my flank, also pulling out. He then gave the distress signal and started for home. He went down in half glide, and I thought his engine had gone dud, and kept alongside him.

I was the first to land, then Nobby, and then Armitage, who made a bumpy landing. When he joined us at the hangar we found he'd been wounded in the leg. It was painful, as the bullet was still there, but nothing very serious, though good enough for a blighty. He was sent off at once to 19 C.C.S. at Agnez, halfway between here and Arras, furious at missing tonight's binge for Joske's M.C.

Three days later:

144

In the afternoon several of us drove over to see Armitage. He'd had an operation, but seemed comfortable, and very cheerful at the prospect of being soon back in England.

Two days after that, on 4 October:

There's been no serious flying for two days, and this afternoon 'C' Flight took the opportunity to go and see Armie again, and take him some chocs and apples, but were surprised to find him looking so ill. The nurse would only allow Nobby and me to see him, and then only for two minutes. She said he'd had another operation and the gas upsets him.

Friday October 5th

Early this morning came the shocking news that Armie died last night of gangrene poisoning. We can't believe it. Although he looked pale yesterday, he seemed cheerful enough, braced at the expectation of soon being sent to England. What on earth could have caused a simple wound like his, under treatment by hospital staff within an hour of it happening, to go wrong so quickly? It made us all very gloomy, as Armie was very popular. We could have taken it better if he'd been killed in a scrap.

Armitage was born on 10 October 1897 and, after attending Ackworth School, was employed as an engineer. He joined the RFC at Oxford in July 1916 and, after training at a variety of units, including 50 (Home Defence) Squadron, arrived at 46 Squadron on 12 June 1917. He died in 19 Casualty Clearing Station.

Robert Leighton Moore Ferrie

This is an illustration of how men continued to fly under the terrible strain of combat, and push themselves on, despite their fears and demons.

Ferrie was born on 7 October 1898 and his father was a publisher in Hamilton, Ontario. He attended the Royal Military College but, at the end of 1916, joined the RFC. Following tuition at a number of reserve squadrons, he arrived at 46 Squadron on 13 June 1917.

Arthur Gould Lee again:

Since Fleming arrived a week ago, we've had four new pilots, and one, Shadwell is married, so I'm no longer on my own. Another, Ferrie, is a Canadian, short and with a cheerful grin. He's a nice fellow, Ferrie, quiet, but as pugnacious as hell.

In July the squadron returned to Sutton's Farm in the UK, to help with the defence of Britain from Gothas based in Belgium, who were causing a significant number of civilian casualties. At the end of August they returned to the Western Front, initially in the Ypres area, and then moved to the Arras area, arriving at Filescamp Farm on 3 September 1917.

The Pup, with which 46 Squadron was equipped, was no match for the

Ferrie's Letter of Identification.

dreaded Albatros. The German machine was much faster, and had two machine guns against the Pup's single Vickers. Their best tactic was to use the low wing loading of the Pup to out-turn the heavy Albatros, as they certainly could not outrun them. The strain of flying operations in an inferior aeroplane would soon tell on anyone's nerves.

Arthur Gould Lee once more:

Nobby is very fed up over Armie's wounding, for we were the only flight still with the same pilots as at Sutton's Farm. He has always looked after us in scraps, as I well know, for he has pulled Huns off my tail two or three times. But Armie's hit was something that could happen at any time - a plucky observer shooting straight. Arnie's replacement, called Warwick, has arrived and the batmen are putting his things in the cubicle behind mine, previously occupied by Ferrie, who has just moved to another hut because we other three in the Nissen groused about the noise he made in nightmares -

146

dreaming his machine was in flames or breaking up, and so on.

On 20 November, the Battle of Cambrai commenced, and 46 were employed on ground strafing, an unpopular task. At least in aerial combat you could see your enemy but ground attack, against countless hidden enemy machine guns, was another matter. A stray bullet through the fuel tank or engine and you stood no chance of regaining the Allied side of the line from very low altitude.

In the middle of December the squadron received a great boost for morale when five MCs were awarded, including Ferrie and Lee. It was during November that, at long last, they realised better equipment was imminent when the first of their Sopwith Camels arrived.

On 3 January 1918 Ferrie led a small patrol of four machines and failed to return. Arthur Gould Lee wrote:

I'm terribly depressed this evening, Ferrie has been killed. He led his patrol out this afternoon, had a scrap, came back leading the others, then as they were flying along quite normally in formation, his right wing suddenly folded back, then the other, and the wreck plunged vertically down. A bullet must have gone through a main spar during the fight.

The others went after him and steered close to him in vertical dives. They could see him, struggling to get clear of his harness, then half standing up. They said it was horrible to watch him trying to decide whether to jump. He didn't, and the machine and he were smashed to nothingness.

I can't believe it. Little Ferrie, with his cheerful grin, one of the finest chaps in the squadron. God, imagine his last moments, seeing the ground rushing up at him, knowing he was a dead man, unable

Camel B2516, delivered to 46 Squadron on 26 November 1917. R L M Ferrie was killed while flying this machine on 3 January 1918. It was also flown by Arthur Gould Lee.

A group of 46 Squadron pilots. Fourth from the left is the commanding officer, Major Babington, the next is R L M Ferrie and eighth from the left is Arthur Gould Lee.

to move, unable to do anything but wait for it. A parachute could have saved him, there's no doubt about that. What the hell is wrong with those callous dolts at home that they won't give them to us?

The remains of the machine were recovered by 15 Squadron and the force of the impact was such that only two cylinders of the engine were undamaged. Ferrie's worst nightmare had, tragically, been realised.

Return to the water tower and continue ahead on the D75E signposted to Avesnes-le-Comte, then the D75. Turn right on the D339 and in the centre of town go right on the D8 towards Beaufort-Blavincourt. The cemetery is on the right. Access is via an entrance in the hedge halfway up the French civilian cemetery.

Avesnes-le-Comte Communal Cemetery Extension

For a period the village was the headquarters of VI Corps. The first two burials were made in the communal cemetery during April 1916, but thereafter they were made in the extension. Four casualty clearing stations were based here and there are now 333 graves of which, unusually, all are identified.

There are 26 fliers in the cemetery (14/35), including two squadron commanders. Again the casualties reflect the location of squadrons, with seven from 12 Squadron, who were based at Avesnes-le-Comte aerodrome, adjacent to the cemetery. There are ten from 11, 29 and 60 Squadrons, who were all based at Le Hameau.

The first grave we are visiting (III C3) is in the plot near the northern end of the burial ground, and is in the front row.

William Arthur Grattan-Bellew (III C3)

Grattan-Bellew was the son of Sir Henry Grattan-Bellew and was born on 15 September 1894. The family lived in western Galway, Ireland. William was educated at Downside and then went up to Cambridge in 1913 to study engineering. He obtained his Royal Aero Club certificate, No. 1039, in January 1915 and shortly afterwards joined the RFC. Three months later, in April, he was posted to 16 Squadron in France and remained with them until June. Unfortunately, he then had to have a hernia operation, the consequence of an appendix operation in 1913. Such was the injury, it was thought he would be unlikely to go on active service again as the problem would be aggravated. Despite this, he was posted to 25 Squadron on 5 October 1915 shortly after they had formed, and then accompanied them to France in February 1916.

Major W A
Grattan-Bellew.

In March he was promoted to flight commander and on 27 July received an MC. Further promotion followed on 5 September, when he was made a major and took command of 29 Squadron. They were operating the DH2 and had a number of successful pilots, including two sergeant pilots, Jack Noakes (later a group captain) and James McCudden, who later, of course, would earn the VC. The DH2 in late 1916 was well past its prime, and on 11 March 1917 new equipment, in the shape of the first six Nieuport Scouts, were delivered to the squadron.

On 21 March Grattan-Bellew took off from Filescamp Farm to deliver the last DH2 to No. 2 Aircraft Depot. Shortly after getting airborne, the engine failed and the aeroplane side-slipped, then dived into the ground.

Grattan-Bellew suffered a compound fracture of the left leg (which had to be amputated) and the right ankle. In addition he fractured his right leg and had concussion. Removed to 37 CCS, he died six hours later from his injuries. He was subsequently Mentioned in Despatches, it being the only recognition, other than the VC, which could be posthumous.

Jimmy McCudden wrote in *Five Years in the Royal Flying Corps:*

I was very sorry to leave 29 Squadron and all the good fellows it contained, and was most of all sorry to bid adieu to my O.C., Major Grattan-Bellew, one of the very best C.O.'s that it has ever been my good fortune to serve under. However, I promised to return to No. 29 Squadron as soon as I came out again.

A fortnight later I heard the awful news that Major Bellew had been killed on 29's last de Havilland, which he was flying back to an aircraft park to exchange for one of the Nieuports with which No. 29 Squadron was re-equipped after I had left. I was so very sorry.

It seems to me that in the Flying Corps the very best fellows are always those who are killed. It is so awful when the good fellows one meets in the R.F.C. are killed in some way or other, that one sits and thinks, "Oh, this damned war and its cursed tragedies." After all, I suppose it is to be, and we cannot alter destiny.

McCudden, of course, had no idea when he wrote this that he would suffer a very similar fate.

Evelyn Paget Graves (I C10)

Major E P Graves.

The next grave we are visiting is in the most southerly plot and is in the second row from the front.

When I came here for the first time the register was missing, so I resorted to walking along each row searching for the grave. I was looking for the very distinctive RAF badge on the headstone but could not find it. I then walked up and down a second time, actually searching for his name. For reasons unknown, though he was serving in the RFC when he was killed, and had been for nearly two and a half years, he has the badge of his parent regiment, the Royal Artillery.

Graves, the son of the Hon. A E P Graves, was born on 5 June 1890 at Pachmarki, India. From 1905 until 1908 he was a student at Lancing College. He obtained his 'ticket', No. 870, within two weeks of the outbreak of war and graduated from CFS on 3 October 1914. Posted to France in March 1915, he was home again three months later. After service in several training units he was sent to 20 Squadron as a flight commander in late December 1915 and accompanied them to France in January 1916. Retuning to the UK five months later, he had another spell with training units, before travelling to 60 Squadron just before Christmas 1916, to take command. They were based at Savy, near Arras, but shortly after his arrival transferred to Filescamp Farm.

At the time activity on this part of the front was increasing, as the British built up their forces for the Battle of Arras.

On 6 March 1917, a four-man flight, including Graves, left on an Offensive Patrol in the Somme river area. Observing eight enemy machines attacking an FE2, they dived on them. In the engagement Captain C T Black saw an aeroplane go down in flames, and when the Nieuports reformed there were only three. An FE was also seen on the ground close to where the first machine crashed. Three FE2s were lost in the area at this time, of which two crews were taken prisoner and one killed. The two fatalities are buried in this cemetery and are: Lieutenant W F W Hills (I C2) and Second Lieutenant W S Gardner (I C12). They were the first crew killed in combat from 57 Squadron since arriving in France on 16 December 1916.

Second Lieutenant G A Giles, another 60 Squadron pilot, wrote in his combat report:

> I was escorting a BE doing photography at Ficheaux when I saw a Nieuport fighting an HA circling round each other below me. I at once went down to assist him and fired a burst and the HA turned towards the lines. I followed firing the whole time. I saw the Nieuport suddenly burst into flames and crash north of Riviere. The HA returned over the lines doing S turns and losing height rapidly. I returned to the BE and then came home to report.

Graves was brought down as the second victory of *Offizierstellvertreter* Wilhelm Cymera of *Jasta 1*. We met Cymera in *Airfields and Airmen, Cambrai* , page 84, when he had an encounter with the legendary Albert Ball. As with Grattan-Bellew, Major Graves was Mentioned in Despatches after his death.

Leslie Oakes Crowther (II B22)

The next casualty in which we are interested is in Plot II, the second most northerly section, and is at the near end of the second row from the back. Crowther was the victim of one of those bizarre accidents that occur in life. His companion that day, Lieutenant Albert Baird Fanstone, described what happened:

> The 6th of December 1916 is a date I shall never forget, the most fateful day of my life. An old school friend of mine had just been posted to No. 8 Squadron and as I had a free afternoon I decided to visit him. I hitched a lift on our unit's tender which happened to be going past La Bellevue on its way to collect supplies. It was a happy reunion, but a short one as my friend was due to carry out a patrol. The tender would not be passing No. 8 Squadron on its return journey for quite some considerable time, so, not wishing to wait about, I telephoned my Flight Commander, Captain L O Crowther, to see if it was possible for a machine to fly over and pick me up. Our Squadron had recently received delivery of a new B.E.2d dual control aircraft which I had already flown by using the controls in the observer's cockpit and as Crowther had not yet had the opportunity to try his hand at the machine he decided to bring the B.E.2d over himself.
>
> Captain Crowther duly arrived in the new B.E.2d (Serial No. 5832) and ordered me into the pilot's cockpit whilst he put himself in the observer's seat. The emergency controls consisted

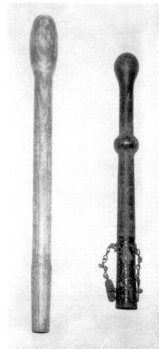

On the left is the actual stick that caused Crowther's death. On the right is the modified version that replaced it. Both were mementoes kept by A B Fanstone.

of a rudder bar and a detachable joystick only, the latter of which, when not in use, was clipped to the side of the cockpit. I took control of the machine to begin with but once we were airborne Crowther signalled to me that he was taking over. All went well until we reached Avesnes aerodrome whereupon he took us round on a circuit of the airfield. The observer's controls did not include the usual flying instruments and in view of both this and the fact Crowther was a very careful pilot, I stood by in readiness, expecting his orders to land the aircraft. The very next instant the nose dropped suddenly and we nose-dived 300 feet into the ground - just missing the officers' mess.

Crowther was killed instantly and I knew nothing further until I came to in a field hospital.

An enquiry followed, the result of which showed that whilst making the initial circuit, the turn that the aircraft was carrying out, coupled with the torque of the engine, had a tendency to pull the nose of the aircraft down. To counteract this Crowther had pulled back on the stick at which point it came right out of its socket, causing him to lose all control. The joystick itself was found some distance from the wreckage and this fact confirmed the findings of the enquiry.

Tragic though Crowther's death had been, it at least brought to light a very serious defect which was immediately remedied and an order was issued grounding the machines until the old control columns had been replaced with metal ones which could be held in place by means of a locking pin.

L O Crowther.

Crowther, born in 1891, had been educated at Malvern College. At the outbreak of war he was living in India and enlisted on 2 September 1914. Obviously anxious to get to the fighting, he came home in October 1915 and obtained a commission in the Royal West Kent Regiment. Joining the RFC he was sent to 29 Squadron on appointment as a flying officer in March 1916 and later in the month crossed to France. On 30 July he moved to 12 Squadron and in November was promoted to flight commander, but was killed only a month later.

152

Fanstone, despite the severity of the crash, was not badly injured, suffering facial injuries, concussion and a sprained left wrist. After a period in England he wangled a posting back to his old squadron, and was immediately involved in the Battle of Arras. In May 1917 he was promoted to flight commander with 8 Squadron, until returning to HE in November. He subsequently served in home defence squadrons and was awarded the Air Force Cross, being demobilised on 24 September 1919. Between the wars, after obtaining an engineering degree from Cambridge, he was a civilian education officer with the RAF. Rejoining the RAF during the Second World War, he spent some time in the USA organising training.

Continue north on the D8 and stop immediately beyond the leaving town sign. The aerodrome was on the right.

Avesnes-le-Comte Aerodrome

The main RFC occupant of this aerodrome was 12 Squadron, who were based here from March 1916 until 9 May 1917. No. 43 Squadron was

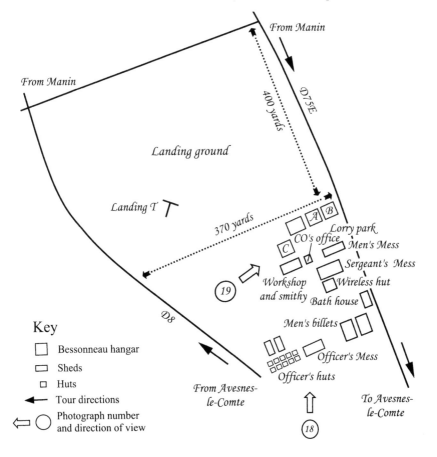

Picture No. 18: Avesnes-le-Comte aerodrome looking north, taken in 2001.

resident from March to June 1918 and 54 Squadron for only a week or so in late 1918. As we have read (page 108), this was where A A McLeod took off from when he earned his VC and is also the spot where the Crowther and Fanstone incident occurred in the previous entry.

R R Money in his book, *Flying and Soldiering*, described the aerodrome:

> Our move to Vert Galand had been a mistake, and now we went to Avesnes Le Comte on the Frevent - Arras road, under Gordon Sheppard (sic.)
>
> The French Artillery were still in position on the Arras front, waiting until our infantry had found their feet, and also until many batteries of our own Artillery could get down from Ypres, where they were being relieved by new batteries from home. A French Artillery Observation Squadron, mounted on Caudrons, remained on the

Picture No. 19: Bristol Scout C5301 of 12 Squadron. These were issued in small numbers to a variety of units. Though delightful to fly they were not really suitable as a fighter.

Avesnes Le Comte aerodrome to look after their gunners until we arrived, and I went over with the C.O. to have a look around and learn a few things before they left. It was my first experience of the French at war, and of the way they ran their flying Squadrons, and I was left a little breathless.

We were billeted in the village to commence with, until a supply of Armstrong huts commenced to arrive and be erected; when first "A" Flight, then "B", and finally "C" Flight, migrated to the aerodrome.

The aerodrome was a very small one, bounded on one side by a road with telegraph wires, on another by a sunken road, and on a third by the hangars, office and a farm-yard. How we got off in our overloaded machine when the ground was wet I do not know. As our old pilots were killed, or went home, their places were taken by others with very little flying experience, and some glorious crashes ensued. The telegraph wires gave way without upsetting a B.E.2C. though they proved strong enough to overturn a Morane and kill the pilot, but the haystacks in the farmyard and the sunken road, cost us several machines.

This aerodrome was one of those that remained unoccupied for long periods. In June 1917, after 12 Squadron had left, there was only one hangar remaining and the grass had grown to such an extent that it would have to be cut before it could be used as a landing ground again.

Return south to the D339 and proceed west to Frévent. In the centre of town turn right on the D54 to Houvin-Houvigneul. Then follow the green War Graves Commission. The right turn to the cemetery is exceedingly sharp. Stop at the first British plot on the right.

St Hilaire Cemetery Extension

Frévent was an important position on the Allied line of communications and a number of casualty clearing stations were established here. During the Second World War it was largely destroyed by bombing, and the civilian cemetery damaged. The Commonwealth War Graves Commission cemetery (13/5) is quite small with only 210 First War burials, plus a dozen Second World War casualties.

This is a curious cemetery, being established on a hill, with the plots being separated by a French military cemetery and a civilian burial ground. It contains two particularly interesting casualties, of which the first (C8), is near the middle of the third row from the far end in the first plot.

Stanley Wallace Rosevear (C8)

A considerable number of Canadians served in the flying services, out of all proportion to their total population. Rosevear was born on 9 March 1896 and came from Port Arthur, Ontario. Joining the RNAS in January 1917, he completed his training at Cranwell (now the RAF College), having done his initial tuition at Crystal Palace and Redcar. Posted to Dover, he shortly joined I Naval, who were attached to the RFC and based at the East Aerodrome, Bailleul (*Ypres*, page 71), equipped with the superb Sopwith Triplane. Rosevear claimed his first victim on 14 August 1917, when he sent an Albatros DV down northeast of Ypres. He scored his eighth victory on 24 October, but in December 1 Naval were withdrawn to Dover and re-equipped with the Camel.

Again, in a letter to Norman Franks, the great Canadian fighter pilot, Ray Collishaw, explained how the navy dealt with battle fatigue:

> While the RFC/RAF used a system of relieving pilots to Home service for a rest after eight or nine months of active duty, the RNAS and the German Jastas had no such system. It was left to the COs to decide when a pilot (or observer) was unable to go on. After a period of ardent work on a 'hot' front, a unit was sent to a 'quiet' sector for a rest.

In December Rosevear was notified that he had been awarded the DSC and on 16 February 1918, 1 Naval returned to the Western Front. In February, March and April, he brought down another fifteen enemy machines. On 20 March he was appointed acting commander of A Flight and in April received a bar to his DSC. Meanwhile, with the formation of the RAF, 1 Naval now ceased to exist and became 201 Squadron, much to the disgust of many RNAS personnel, who lamented the loss of their naval traditions and terminology.

On 22 April Rosevear shot down his twenty-fifth victim, a Pfalz DIII. Three days later, while diving on a practice target during a test flight, he inexplicably flew straight into the ground. A possible reason was fixation on a ground object which has caused countless pilots to leave their pull up too late. Admitted to 19 CCS, he died an hour later of a fractured lower spine.

His headstone has no cross engraved on it and, curiously, there is no indication of the bar to his DSC.

Samuel James Mitchell and the Air Force Medal (B3)

The next grave (B3) is in the next row in front of Rosevear. In *Airfields and Airmen, Somme*, page 161, the institution of separate awards for the new Royal Air Force was explained. The Distinguished Flying Medal was awarded to other ranks and non commissioned officers for noteworthy actions on operations but the Air Force Medal was for good work of a non-

156

operational kind, such as test flying or training. The DFC and AFC, for commissioned officers and warrant officers, were awarded in the same way.

Like the DFM, only about 100 AFMs were awarded during the war, with possibly only two bars and again only one recipient is buried on the Western Front.

Mitchell was born in May 1896 and was the third of seven children. In 1910 he started training as a patternmaker and remained in this employment after war was declared. On 26 October 1915 he enlisted in the RFC as a second class air mechanic and was promoted to sergeant on 8 July 1917. In early 1917 he commenced pilot training and after a number of different units he was posted to 11 Squadron in France at the beginning of September 1917. They were based at La Bellevue (see page 172) and were operating Bristol Fighters. He was

Mitchell (right) with his brother.

The form sent to Mitchell's father in August 1920 by the Imperial War Graves Commission (as it was then) asking him to confirm the details for his son's headstone. This may explain why there is no AFM inscribed on the stone as the IWGC failed to record it and the omission was not corrected by his father. On the right is the epitaph requested by the family.

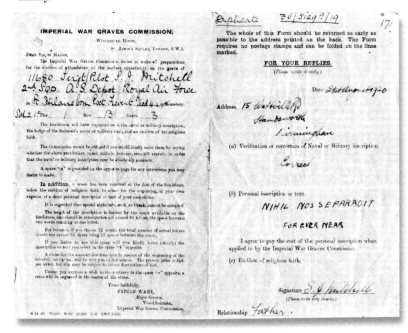

The memorabilia of S J Mitchell held by his family. It includes his Royal Aero Club certificate, flying logbook, death plaque and medals. His AFM has the later diagonal striped ribbon.

only with them for a short time before being posted back to the UK. He re-embarked for France on 19 October and was posted to No. 2 Aeroplane Supply Depot at Candas, southwest of Doullens as a ferry pilot. Much of his work involved delivering machines to 100 Squadron, part of the Independent Force down on the French sector, which involved long and arduous flights. It was for this invaluable work that he was awarded his Air Force Medal.

On the morning of 3 April 1918 Mitchell left No. 2 Aeroplane Supply Depot at Fienvillers in Bristol Fighter C794. While landing at 80 Squadron's aerodrome at Belleville Farm, northwest of Doullens, he hit a bank and crashed, following which the machine caught fire. Admitted to No. 3 Canadian CCS with burns to body, arms, leg and buttocks, Mitchell died of his injuries the following day. His Commonwealth War Graves headstone does not record the fact he was awarded the AFM.

His passenger, Flight Sergeant John Edward O'Shea MSM, survived but was badly burned. He lost most of the use of his right eye and on discharge from hospital in January 1919 had scars on his face and hands. Born in Ladywood, Warwick, O'Shea had joined the RFC in October 1915. Crossing to France on 17 March 1916 he appears to have been employed at No. 2 Aircraft Depot and No. 2 Aeroplane Supply Depot from that date until his accident. He was promoted to flight sergeant in March 1918. Apart from receiving the Meritorious Service Medal he was also Mentioned in Despatches. Upon discharge from the RAF on 16 January 1919, he was awarded an additional sixpence a day disability pension on account of his gallant conduct.

For a fuller account of Mitchell's life I recommend an excellent article by Peter Wright in *Cross and Cockade International*, volume nineteen, page 138.

Return to the centre of town. At the D916 go straight across and follow Toutes Directions to a roundabout then turn right to the D941 to Hesdin and Auxi-le-Chateau. Continue on the D941 to Auxi. You will pass a sign to Boffles, which was the aerodrome James McCudden was trying to find. Continue through Auxi and just after leaving the village sign turn right to Neuilly-le-Dien. Climb the hill through the wood and stop at the top at an unmarked crossroad next to the Pas-de-Calais/Somme Département boundary sign. The aerodrome is on your left.

Auxi-le-Chateau Aerodrome

This site was one chosen during the German advance of March 1918, when the RFC had to abandon some of its forward aerodromes. The first unit based here was No.8 Squadron, who arrived on 6 April 1918 with their Armstrong Whitworth Big Acks. They were joined by 52 Squadron on 30 June, operating the RE8.

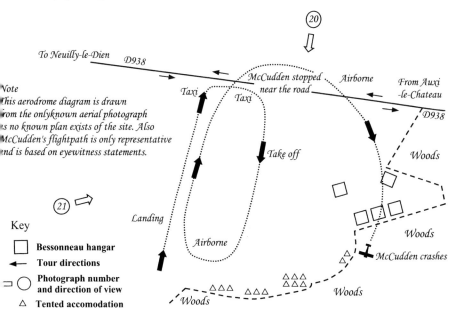

159

Picture No. 20: Auxi-le-Chateau in 1918 looking south.

Picture No.21: Auxi-le-Chateau in 2003 looking northeast.

The fatal crash of James McCudden VC

Both units were still based here on the late afternoon of 9 July, when an unknown SE5a landed in order to ask for directions. Shortly after, it took off and crashed. A witness was 134791 Corporal W Howard, a Royal Army Medical Corps orderly with 8 Squadron:

An S.E.5a aeroplane landed on this aerodrome at about 5.40 pm on Tuesday, 9th July, and after a few minutes took off again. I saw the machine pass over the wood adjoining the aerodrome and immediately afterwards heard a crash. I immediately ran to the spot and was the first to reach the machine. It was badly wrecked and I found the pilot unconscious but still breathing. His rank was Major and he wore the V.C. and other decorations. I was afterwards informed that he was Major McCudden. I and other men placed him on a stretcher and took him as quickly as possible to 21 CCS.

McCudden was found bleeding profusely from the mouth and nose. He died of his injuries, a severe fracture of the base of the skull and jaw, two hours later. Many of the top aces of the First World War died in mysterious circumstances and the way in which McCudden met his demise is no exception. Speculation as to why he crashed continues to this day.

There were a number of aircrew witnesses from both squadrons and though most agree, in certain important areas they do not. All agree that the machine was flying east at about 200 feet. Two of them mention the engine running roughly and two that the engine stopped before the machine hit the trees. One suggested he had been stunting (rolling) and another that the machine completed one roll to the right before crashing. Two stated that a very steep or vertical turn was made near the ground.

It was unlikely that McCudden was showing off with a display of aerobatics, as he was not that sort of pilot, having a very disciplined approach to flying and, in addition, had no audience to impress. Undoubtedly, his mind would have been focussed on reaching nearby Boffles, where he was to take command of 60 Squadron. The most likely cause was that he suffered a power loss shortly after take off and, in trying to avoid crashing into the trees, stalled the aeroplane, which started a spin at too low an altitude for a recovery to be made.

There has been much criticism as to the lack of ceremony or publicity for one of Britain's most decorated heroes after he was killed. Corporal Howard's statement was not made until 18 July, nine days after the crash, and the accident report was not completed until 14 July, five day later.

It was such a sad end for such an accomplished flier. He was on the brink of a whole new chapter in his life, with the command of his own squadron, but lost his life in a simple accident.

For an account of McCudden's life see the next section in this book.

Retrace your steps on the D941 to Auxi and then follow the D938 to Doullens. After the Beauvoir-Wavans village sign you will see the green War Graves Commission sign on your left. Follow the track to the cemetery.

Wavans British Cemetery

I have been here many times over the years and it is my favourite cemetery (8/1) on the Western Front. It is small and in the middle of nowhere, far from the front lines, a beautiful, quiet place. Utilised by 21 CCS from May until September 1918, it contains only 43 Commonwealth burials and a solitary German, all of whom are identified. Surprisingly, for such a small cemetery, twelve are flyers, of whom two were top scoring aces of the RAF.

Major J T B McCudden VC (B10)

The grave we have come to pay our respects to is on the right hand end of the second row and contains the remains of one of the greatest fighter pilots of the First World War. He is one of my heroes and on every visit to the cemetery I am deeply moved.

McCudden was born on 28 March 1895, one of four sons of a corporal in the Royal Engineers, of whom three were to be killed while flying. Educated in army schools, he joined the Royal Engineers as a boy soldier on 26 April 1910 and was re-graded as a bugler six months later. In 1913 he was accepted into the RFC as a second class air mechanic. Despite having no formal engineering training, his enthusiasm and curiosity in all mechanical things gave him a sound knowledge of engines. In June 1913 he was posted to No. 3 Squadron where he never lost an opportunity to fly as a passenger. He moved to France with 3 Squadron on 13 August 1914 and in May 1915 recognition of his abilities was rewarded with promotion to sergeant in charge of all engine maintenance in the unit. Continuing to fly as much as possible, including some unofficial pilot instruction, he re-mustered as an observer. After a number of engagements with the enemy,

Jimmy McCudden (centre), wearing a peaked cap with the personnel from his flight in 56 Squadron.

McCudden received the French *Croix de Guerre.*

In January McCudden got his wish and returned to the UK for pilot training. After tuition at Gosport, he obtained his Royal Aero Club 'ticket', No. 2745, on 16 April 1916. On completion of his training he was posted to 20 Squadron, who were flying the ungainly, but effective, FE2 from Clairmarais, near St Omer. He was only with them a month before he achieved his ambition and was transferred to 29 Squadron, a fighter unit, a few miles to the east. They were flying the DH2 and on 6 September 1916 he scored his first victory. He had a number of indecisive engagements and received the Military Medal before being promoted from sergeant to second lieutenant. By February 1917 he had claimed five victories and received the MC, but on the 23rd was posted home.

After a number of training appointments, where one of his pupils was his younger brother, and another Mick Mannock, he returned to France in command of B Flight of 56 Squadron. This was Ball's old squadron but McCudden's attitude to air fighting was completely different. Where Ball would attack anything, regardless of odds, McCudden's keen and analytical mind viewed each situation from a tactical point. Never afraid to attack he would, nevertheless, withdraw from a fight if it was disadvantageous. He was determined that his flight would be the best and he imposed meticulous maintenance standards on his ground crews and pressed the need for teamwork. On 18 August 1917 McCudden claimed his first victory with 56 Squadron, sending an Albatros scout spinning down out of control. In the next two days he claimed three more.

On 23 September 1917 McCudden's flight, together with C Flight, were involved in one of the best known aerial battles of the Great War, when the great ace Werner Voss was shot down and killed (*Ypres*, page 162). McCudden spent a lot of time refining his aeroplane and honing his skills. In December he was awarded the DSO. During December 56 Squadron had claimed eighteen German machines, of which McCudden's share was fourteen! In January a bar to his DSO was promulgated. On 1 March 1918 McCudden flew his last sortie in 56 Squadron. In just five months he had claimed 52 enemy aircraft, 40% of the squadron total.

British victory claims

Within the First World War aviation research fraternity there has been considerable discussion, if not heated argument, in recent years over RFC/RNAS/RAF claims and victory scores. The French and the German air services not only recognised their victorious fighter pilots but encouraged them. The awarding of the German *Pour le Mérite* was based on a fighter pilot's total number of victories, with the requisite number being raised as the war progressed. The French were probably the most conscientious and demanding nation, with victories having to be witnessed and generally on their side of the lines.

The British never officially recognised the ace system though, as in McCudden's VC citation, total numbers of claims were quoted. In combat reports squadron commanders would classify claims as either decisive or indecisive. Fighting mostly on the other side of the lines, British and Empire pilots did not have the luxury of following a victim to the ground because they were in danger of being pounced upon and shot down. Neither did they have the wreckage to confirm their claim. The name of the game was aerial supremacy, and to force an opponent out of a combat or drive him down out of control was enough. Even the RFC Communiqués (known as *Comic Cuts,* after a popular magazine of the day), which recorded the daily work of the air service, were an intelligence summary. It was neither confirming nor cataloguing fighter pilots claims, but just reviewing how the air war was going.

There was gross over-claiming, much as there was in the Second World War, but it is the perception of the different systems of calculating victories that have caused many modern aviation historians to lose sight of the plot.

In McCudden's case he is certainly the most verifiable of all the British aces. Apart from his official duties as flight commander, he also flew many solo sorties in pursuit of high flying German observation machines. With his highly tuned and adjusted machine, he was able to fly at the altitudes these machines flew at. Of his 57 claims, nineteen were brought down on the Allied side of the lines. This sort of flying was gruelling in the extreme. Did you need to do additional patrols in excess of one's duty? Flying at 20,000 feet in an open cockpit, in arctic temperatures and suffering the effects of anoxia, really demonstrate McCudden's devotion to duty and determination.

On 5 March 1918 McCudden returned home, and in the London Gazette of 29 March 1918 his VC citation was published:

For most conspicuous bravery, exceptional perseverance, keenness and very high devotion to duty. Captain McCudden has at the present time accounted for 54 enemy aeroplanes. Of these 42 have been definitely destroyed, 19 of them on our side of the lines. Only 12 out of the 54 have been driven out of control. On two occasions he has totally destroyed four two-seater enemy aeroplanes on the same day, and on the last occasion all four machines were destroyed in the space of 1 hour and 30 minutes. While in his present squadron he has participated in 78 offensive patrols, and in nearly every case has been the leader. On at least 30 other occasions, whilst with the same squadron, he has crossed the lines alone, either in pursuit or in quest of enemy aeroplanes. The following incidents are examples of the work he has done recently. On the 23rd December 1917, when leading his patrol, eight enemy aeroplanes were attacked between 2.30 p.m. and 3.50 p.m. Of these two were shot down by Captain McCudden in our lines. On the morning of the same day he left the ground at 10.50 and encountered four enemy aeroplanes; of these he shot two down. On 30th January, 1918, he, single-handed, attacked five enemy scouts, as a result of which two were destroyed. On this occasion he only returned home when the enemy scouts had been driven far east; his Lewis gun ammunition was all finished and the belt of his Vickers gun had broken. As a patrol leader he has at all times shown the utmost gallantry and skill, not only in the manner in which he has attacked and destroyed the enemy, but in the way he has during several aerial fights protected the new members of his flight, thus keeping down their casualties to a minimum. This officer is considered, by the record which he has made, by his fearlessness, and by the great service which he has rendered to his country, deserving of the very highest honour.

He served at the No. 1 School of Aerial Fighting School at Ayr in Scotland for a period and was then advised he would be taking 91 Squadron to France as commanding officer. It was to be some while before they would be ready for operations, so he pressed for an immediate return to operational flying. He was given command of 60 Squadron and the days before he departed were extremely busy. During his time at the Fighting School he had written his autobiography which he handed to C G Grey, editor of the aviation magazine weekly *The Aeroplane*. He also prepared his new SE5a and on 9 July 1918 departed from Hounslow. He landed briefly at Hesdin and then took off again for Boffles, where 60 Squadron was stationed. Landing at Auxi-le-Chateau he asked two mechanics directions for Boffles and was then tragically killed in a simple accident.

It is interesting to speculate what would have happened if McCudden had survived. He may very well have been the top scoring ace of the war. He was a calculating tactician and was not one for rashly rushing headlong into a situation. As a professional soldier, his abilities would almost certainly have propelled him to the highest ranks of the RAF. His career, though short, is outstanding. In a class-ridden society and army, in just four years McCudden had risen from air mechanic first class to major and, was arguably, the most decorated member of the British armed forces.

Whenever I return to Wavans and stand in front of McCudden's grave I wonder what might have been. I am particularly fond of the epitaph on his headstone:

Fly on, dear boy
From this world of strife
On to the promised land
To eternal life

Robert Alexander Little (D7)

Just two rows behind McCudden is another great ace, R A Little. The visitor will notice that he has the naval fouled anchor on his headstone.

Little was born on 19 July 1895 at Hawthorn, Melbourne. When war broke out he was attending Scotch College in Melbourne. Anxious to fly, he was unable to get a place on the first Point Cook military flying school course, as there were several hundred applicants for just four places. At his own expense, he sailed for England and learned to fly with the London and Provincial Aviation Company at Hendon and gained his 'ticket', No.1512, on 27 October 1915. Joining the

R A Little.

RNAS on 14 January 1916 as a temporary flight-sub-lieutenant, he was sent to Eastchurch on the Thames Estuary for military flying training. His early career got off to a poor start and he came perilously close to having his commission terminated.

> As an officer he is quite hopeless & likely to remain so. As a pilot he displays considerable courage & keenness, although lacking in skill.

His cause was not helped by crashing an Avro on 14 May 1916, when he hit a dyke at Eastchurch. At one stage it was being suggested that his talents would be better employed flying seaplanes.

> As soon as he learns to be less irresponsible, & when flying to use his head to better advantage, I shall feel confident that he will do exceptionally well on Active Service.

Fortunately for him and the RNAS, his superiors could see potential, and a year later his report read:

> A most loyal capable & keen young officer with few, if any equals as a fighting pilot.

The reason for this dramatic change in his fortunes was that, in October 1916, he had been posted to 8 Naval, who were flying Pups. On 23 November he shot down an enemy two-seater in flames and the following month claimed two more victories. In January 1917 the squadron exchanged their Pups for Sopwith Triplanes. By the middle of July, he had shot down twenty-four German aircraft and been awarded a DSC. The Triplanes were in turn replaced by the Camel and by the time he was rested from operations at the end of July he had claimed 38 victories and been awarded a bar to his DSC and a DSO. In August he received a bar to his DSO, having also been awarded the French *Croix de Guerre*.

Tich Rochford, another notable naval ace, wrote of Little in his book, *I Chose the Sky:*

> He was a deadly accurate marksman both in the air and on the

Little's Triplane N5493 in which he claimed twenty victories while with 8 Naval at Mont-St-Éloi.

ground and carried a revolver which he always took with him into the air. With it he practiced on rats around the camp. He was also, apparently, a very capable performer with a .22 sporting rifle as Ron Sykes recalls; 'Captain Little, my Flight Commander, aimed to be the fastest gun on the Western Front through regular practice with his 22 rifle! Walking with him round the aerodrome, looking for a target and not finding one, I threw my RN cap into the air like a clay-pigeon and said, 'You can't hit that'.

'But he did and my cap had that bullet-hole through it ever after'.

Home service was not to Little's liking and he was soon agitating for a return to operations. In this he was successful, being posted to 3 Naval, commanded by Ray Collishaw, as a flight commander.

On 1 April 1918, the day 3 Naval became 203 Squadron RAF, he made his first claim in his new unit. They moved to Filescamp Farm (see page 140) on 16 May and on the 22nd Little claimed his 47th and last victory, a DFW two-seater.

Tich Rochford again:

Great fighter pilot though he was - he won the DSO and bar, the DSC and bar and the Croix de Guerre - Little had another side to his character which was not of war. He loved nature and had a small flower garden close to his hut. His remarkable eyesight and powers of observation would be demonstrated if one took a walk with him in the countryside. He could pick out animal trails that his companion had missed.

Tich Rochford described Little's last flight:

Not long after darkness had fallen on the night of 27th May, I was in the mess drinking and talking with other pilots of our squadron. We heard the engines of a German raider as it passed overhead. Little left the mess and soon afterwards the familiar sound of a Bentley rotary reached our ears from the direction of the aerodrome. The noise temporarily faded as the Camel taxied away from the hangars, then became louder as on full-throttle it took off

*into dark night. Later Kiwi Beamish came into the mess and
confirmed that Little had gone up in his Camel - not for the first time
- to attack the German bombers. Three hours passed by and there
was still no sign of Little's return. His fuel supply must have been
long since exhausted but no message had come through reporting
his landing elsewhere.*

*After some hours had passed, Major Booker of No. 201 Squadron
telephoned to say that a Camel had been found completely wrecked
near Noeux with the body of the dead pilot lying beside it. Booker
had gone at once to the scene of the crash and identified the body as
that of Little whom he knew very well as they had been together in
8 Naval during 1917.*

*From the wrecked condition of his machine it seems probable
that Little was either dead or unconscious at the moment of impact.
At some time prior to this he had been wounded in the thigh by a
single bullet. He was officially reported to have died from wounds
and shock. The full story of Little's tragic last flight that night will
never be known, but he must have been wounded by the return fire
of a gunner when attacking an EA.*

*Robert Alexander Little, one of the bravest men I have known,
loved air fighting and was quite without fear.*

Like McCudden and many other top aces, Little died in mysterious
circumstances. He left a widow and small son. Today he rests in the quiet
solitude of Wavans cemetery.

**Continue on the D938 to Doullens and at the D925 go left into Doullens for
the N25. Follow the green War Graves Commission sign to the left.
Approaching the civilian cemetery turn left to follow the red brick cemetery
wall and park at the end on the left.**

Doullens Communal Cemetery Extension No. 2

Doullens was Marshal Foch's headquarters early in the war and where
the conference was held in March 1918, in which he was appointed
supremo of all the Allied armies on the Western Front. It was an important
railhead, and when the area was taken over from the French by the British,
a number of casualty clearing stations were established. From February
1916 until April 1918, the British medical units buried their dead in the
French extension (No. 1). With the German advance of spring 1918, a
severe strain was put on the stationary hospital here and the extension was
filled. A new extension (No. 2) was opened on the other side of the French
communal cemetery. There are now 350 First World War burials or

commemorations in this extension (8/2). The two graves (I B28 and I B29) we have come to see are in the second row on the left and are the fourth and fifth graves along.

In *Airfields and Airmen, Somme*, I put a request for anyone to contact me who had more information on any of the entries in the book and also anybody who had relatives in the flying services during the Great War. The response has been very gratifying and since then I have had over twenty contacts.

Mond and Martyn, the sequel (I B28 and I B29)

One of these was from Brian Sperring (a former British Airways pilot), who had more information concerning the Mond and Martyn entry in *Airfields and Airmen, Somme* (see page 132.) He knew May, the younger sister of Francis Mond, until she died some years ago and she had notes concerning her mother's quest for her son's grave. I was then put in touch with Dan Cippico, Mond's nephew, who had a large collection of memorabilia, which he has generously allowed me to use.

Francis Mond did indeed serve with 16 Squadron during 1915 but returned to England after a crash. Following categorisation as unfit to fly he served for the next eighteen months on staff duties. After refresher flying he arrived at 57 Squadron on 3 April 1918 and was posted to C Flight.

The air battle in which Mond and Martyn were killed was witnessed by men of 31st Battalion Australian Infantry, who gallantly went out under shell-fire and brought their bodies in. Lieutenant Harold Hill, who was in charge of the party, had rescued another pilot in broad daylight well into No Man's Land only five days before. For these actions he was awarded a Bar to his MC. Mond and Martyn were identified and their personal possessions returned to the squadron. Both bodies were very badly mutilated around the head. They were sent down river by boat and left in charge of Sergeant Major Hempel of 6 Australian Field Ambulance, at an

Mond's Royal Aero Club certificate, No. 1197, issued on 22 April 1915.

The remains of Mond and Martyn's DH4 photographed after the war.

advanced dressing station known as Smith's Farm. The stretcher bearers who had brought the bodies down saw them still there 24 hours later. Three days later, the same stretcher bearers noticed the bodies had gone. In the meantime Hempel, who had been awaiting a lorry to come and retrieve them had, while walking down the Corbie road, encountered an RAF lorry. Believing it to be the vehicle from 57 Squadron, he handed over the two dead airmen and was given a receipt.

After the war Mrs Mond began exhaustive enquiries regarding the fate of her son. She circularised and in many cases interviewed all officers and NCOs serving in 5 Brigade RAF at the time. She contacted the two stretcher bearers and Hempel, who confirmed that the bodies were the only two aviators who had passed through the ADS while he was in charge. All these enquiries failed to provide any further information.

At the end of 1921 Mrs Mond's attention was drawn to a case being examined by the Air Ministry Casualty Department. It concerned a crew from 11 Squadron, Captain J V Aspinall and his observer, Second Lieutenant P V de la Cour, who were also lost on 15 May 1918 and were buried at Doullens. They were reported to have been shot down in flames well on the German side of the lines. In addition the only items returned to Aspinall's family were objects found in his billet and none of de la Cour's personal effects were ever returned.

Mrs Mond found the names of all NCOs in 11 Squadron and circularised them. She found the two men who had brought the bodies back and they independently stated that they had taken a Crossley Tender to Smith's Farm and collected two unrecognisable bodies from an *Australian* sergeant major. The bodies were returned to 11 Squadron and buried in good faith as their two dead officers.

With all her evidence assembled, Mrs Mond presented it to the War Graves Commission. In 1923 one body was exhumed at Doullens in the presence of Mrs Mond and the father of J V Aspinall. It was identified as that of Mond and the other grave was opened and identified as Martyn. The feelings of Mrs Mond are unimaginable, as are those of the families of Aspinall and de la Cour, whose sons suddenly now had unknown burial places. Both Aspinall and de la Cour are commemorated on the Air Forces Memorial to the Missing at Arras.

Francis Mond had a great interest in aviation and in 1919 Emile, Francis' father, endowed the Francis Mond Chair of Aeronautical Engineering at Cambridge University. (Emile's brother Albert, later Lord Melchett, was a founder of ICI.)

170

The diligence and fortitude of Angela Mond was incredible and in the end she was able to achieve her aim, an honoured known grave for her beloved lost son.

Johann Janzen

Mond and Martyn were brought down by *Leutnant* Johann Janzen of *Jasta* 6 as his fifth victory. Born on 21 May 1896, he volunteered for service with the 1st *Leibhusaren* Regiment on 3 August 1914. After service in Russia, he was transferred to the Western Front, but bored with life with the cavalry he transferred to the air service in April 1916. Following training he was posted to *Kagohl* 1 on the Eastern Front. They returned to France and Janzen's *staffel* re-equipped with the twin-engined Gotha machine, of which he was not very fond. He was very relieved when his *staffelführer* was given the task of establishing *Jasta* 23, and Janzen went with him.

The unit was posted to the French front and, on 14 February 1917, claimed its first victory, a French observation balloon. Janzen scored his first victory on 25 February. In August Janzen's commanding officer was posted to a two-seater unit, and the *jasta* was designated a Bavarian unit. A change was felt in order by Janzen and he managed to obtain a posting to *Jasta* 6, part of *Jagdgeschwader* 1, in the Courtrai area opposite the British. After four victories, Janzen was appointed to command *Jasta* 4, whose commanding officer had been seriously wounded. This was a retrograde step, as they were equipped with old Pfalz DIIIs, whereas Janzen's previous *jasta* were operating the Fokker Triplane. Unable to score any victories, he was fortunately given command of *Jasta* 6 and returned to flying Triplanes again.

Johann Janzen wearing his Iron Cross 1st Class and pilot's badge.

Janzen in front of his Fokker Triplane. Mond and Martyn were his sixth victory.

On 9 June 1918, now flying a Fokker DVII, he engaged in a fight with several French Spads and, while trying to shoot one down, his gun interrupter gear malfunctioned and he shot his own propeller off. At too low a height to re-cross the lines, he was taken prisoner. By this time he had claimed thirteen victories. In December he escaped and was able to reach Germany. It is believed he died in the 1980s.

Return to the main road. Turn right on the N25 to Arras. In La Bellevue turn left on the D25 to Couturelle. After a short distance, at the junction of the D25 and the D127 to Humbercourt, turn round and park. The aerodrome was situated around the farm to the east of you.

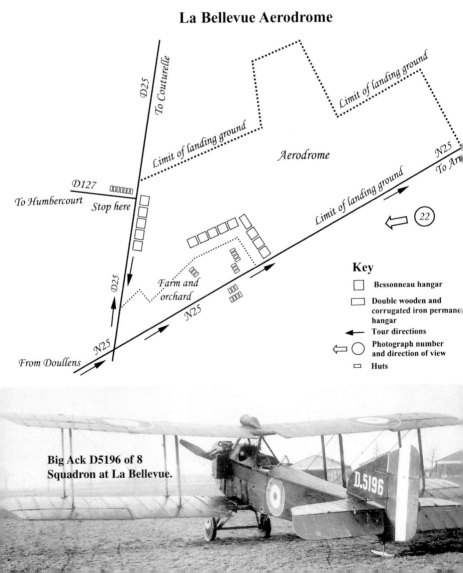

La Bellevue Aerodrome

Big Ack D5196 of 8 Squadron at La Bellevue.

Picture No. 22: La Bellevue in 2003 looking west.

This aerodrome was in continuous operational use from February 1916 until May 1919. No. 8 Squadron was the first unit to arrive and, purely by chance, was also the last unit to be based here. Other RFC/RAF squadrons that used it were 2, 11, 18, 32, 35, 49, 59, 60, 62, 73 and 80.

The Bristol Fighter

The Bristol F2b was one of the truly great designs of the war and soldiered on with the RAF until the 1930s, but its debut into active service was a disaster, as will be seen in the next section.

Designed by Frank Barnwell, the Bristol F2a was powered by a 190 hp Rolls-Royce Falcon. The prototype flew on 9 September 1916 and initially the machine had modified BE2c main-planes. It was quickly ordered and put into production, with the first ten delivered by the end of the year. Production machines had a newly designed wing. In early 1917, 48 Squadron began receiving the first F2as, as their BE12s were withdrawn

Bristol F2a A3322 '5' of 48 Squadron, missing on 13 April, nine days after the Leefe Robinson disaster. Second Lieutenants H D Davies and R S L Worsley were taken prisoner.

to keep 19 and 21 Squadrons up to strength in France. The squadron crossed to France on 8 March 1917 but was held back to achieve maximum surprise when the Battle of Arras began in April.

Meanwhile the second prototype F2a underwent a modification programme to improve pilot visibility and enhance the lift effect of the lower centre section, plus other changes. The first 150 F2b machines, as they were designated, were fitted with the 190 hp Falcon 1, but later the 220 hp Falcon II was installed and then, finally, the 275 hp Falcon III. A decision was made to standardise all fighter-reconnaissance units on the Bristol Fighter (as it was always known) and between May and August 1917, 11, 20 and 22 Squadrons replaced their FE2s with it. Eventually, 62 and 88 Squadrons received the type as well.

48 Squadron and William Leefe Robinson VC

The squadron was formed on 15 April 1916 at Netheravon from a nucleus of 7 Reserve Squadron and in June moved base to Rendcomb. On 9 February they received a new flight commander, Captain William Leefe Robinson VC.

Robinson was born on 14 July 1895 at South Coorg in India, where his father was a coffee planter. He was the youngest of seven children and at the age of fourteen went with his brother Harold to St Bees School in Cumberland. He quickly became a popular figure and was made captain of his house, captain of the school rugby team, a prefect and sergeant in the school Officers' Training Corps. From St Bees he entered Sandhurst, very shortly after war was declared, and was commissioned into the 5/Worcester Regiment. After only three months he transferred to the RFC as an observer and went to France to join 4 Squadron. Unfortunately, his career was short, as on 9 May he was wounded in the right arm and

William Leefe Robinson.

invalided to the UK.

After pilot training and receiving his RFC 'wings' he was posted to 39 (Home Defence) Squadron at Sutton's Farm. This was later renamed Hornchurch and was one of the important fighter stations during the Battle of Britain. They were flying BE2s adapted for night flying, though these modifications were fairly rudimentary by today's standards, and in an age preceding radar or radio the chance of finding a target at night was pretty slim. On the night of 25/26 April 1916 Leefe Robinson sighted a Zeppelin but was unable to climb to its height and he had to open fire at extreme range. The airship simply released ballast and climbed out of danger.

The Germans mounted their largest raid during the night of 2/3 September 1916, when twelve naval and four army airships set out to bomb London. One of the army airships was the Schutte Lanz SL11, commanded by *Hauptmann* Wilhelm Emil Ludwig Schramm who,

The burnt out remains of SL11.

ironically, had been born in London, when his father had been a representative for the German Siemens company.

Schramm dropped a number of bombs across Hertfordshire and the machines of the home defence squadrons took off to intercept. Robinson saw one Zeppelin and made a course to cut off its return track, but lost it in cloud. He returned to his patrol line and on seeing a red glow on the ground, headed towards it. He then spotted a Zeppelin illuminated by searchlights. He dived on it and expended two drums of Lewis gun ammunition with no effect. Closing to 500 feet, he fired his last drum into the airship's belly. The area began to glow and shortly the whole airship was engulfed in fire, descending vertically, then falling into a field at Cuffley, southeast of Hatfield in Hertfordshire. Robinson, low on fuel landed at Sutton's Farm at 0245 hours. To a population who had suffered under the bombing from these supposedly invincible airships, the sight of the fiery end of SLII was a tremendous boost to confidence and morale.

On 5 September Robinson's VC was officially promulgated, an unprecedented short time for the award of this decoration to be announced. At a special investiture in Windsor Castle just *three* days later, King George V presented him with his VC. The importance of countering the Zeppelin menace is perhaps reflected in the amazingly short time the formalities of Robinsons' award occurred. He was a national hero and, despite his reluctance, was mobbed wherever he went. Tiring of this attention, he pleaded for a posting away from the public eye. In February 1917 he was posted to 48 Squadron, due to take the new Bristol Fighter to war.

On 8 March 48 Squadron moved to France and arrived at La Bellevue. Just a month later, on 5 April 1917, they mounted their first operational sortie. The six inexperienced Bristols had the terrible misfortune to encounter the very experienced pilots of Manfred von Richthofen's *Jasta* 11. Of the six, four were lost, and on returning from prisoner of war camp on 14 December 1918, Robinson made this statement:

175

On OP over Douai, flying in formation. Attacked by enemy formation. Had considerable trouble with my machine gun which kept jamming. Engine shot and forced to land. Unwounded. Turned machine over landing and burnt it.

The Bristols had been operated in the traditional style of two-seaters, where the pilot positioned the aeroplane in order to give his gunner the opportunity to use the rear gun. Once the speed and manoeuvrability of the new machine had been appreciated, tactics were changed. The Bristol was then flown aggressively, like a fighter, with the pilot using his forward firing gun with the gunner covering the tail. There were a number of high scoring aces who flew the Bristol fighter, including W E Staton who features on page 183.

During captivity Robinson received harsh treatment and, after a couple of escape attempts, he was sent to the notorious Holzminden camp, commanded by Karl Niemeyer (*Somme*, page 61). For his services during captivity Robinson was Mentioned in Despatches. By the time he returned from prisoner of war camp, on 14 December 1918, he was a sick man and on 31 December he succumbed to heart failure, brought on by the virulent influenza virus that was sweeping Europe. He was buried at All Saints Church in Harrow Weald, Middlesex on 3 January 1919.

Robinson and his observer, Second Lieutenant E D Warburton, were brought down by *Vizefeldwebel* Sebastian Festner, as his fourth victory.

Vizefeldwebel Sebastian Festner

Born on 30 June 1894 at Holzkirchen, Bavaria, Festner was a mechanic with *Flieger Abteilung* 1 in late 1914. With this unit and later *FA* 7b he was able to get some unofficial pilot tuition. After official training he was briefly posted to *FA* 18 and *FA* 5b before arriving at *Jasta* 11 on 10 November 1916. He made his first claim on 5 February 1917, a BE2. In Bloody April he claimed ten British machines, earning the Iron Cross First Class and was only the second recipient of the Member's Cross with Swords of the Royal Hohenzollern House Order. This was awarded only two days before his death, which occurred on 25 April. He was noted as fighting four BE machines and crashed near Gavrelle. There were theories that he may have been hit by ground fire or his propeller broke. However, Lieutenants C R O'Brien and J L Dickson of 43 Squadron, flying a Sopwith 11/2 Strutter, shot down a red Albatros, and may have been the likely victors.

Sebastian Festner.

Return to the N25 and proceed towards Arras. In Beaumetz-les-Loges turn right onto the D7 to Rivière and Bapaume. Go left on the D34 to Rivière and Grosville which becomes the D30 to Wailly. At the T junction, turn left onto the D3 to Wailly. Proceed through Wailly to Agny and then turn right onto the D60 to Agny. Pass through Agny on the D60 and over two roundabouts then turn right on the D5 to Neuville-Vitasse. (At the second roundabout there are signs to the Commonwealth War Graves Commission headquarters for France and Switzerland). The cemetery is on the right hand side.

London Cemetery, Neuville-Vitasse

The village of Neuville-Vitasse was captured on 9 April 1917 during the Battle of Arras, by the 56th (London) Division. The cemetery (10/12) was started by this unit and was greatly expanded after the Armistice by bringing in battlefield casualties and bodies from other cemeteries. There are 747 graves or commemorations here, of which 318 are unidentified.

Such was the ferocity of the fighting in this vicinity that there are five panels at the rear of the burial ground bearing the names of casualties who were buried in four cemeteries which were subsequently destroyed by shell fire, and whose graves have been lost. It is one of these casualties who we are interested in. The name of Stephen Dendrino is engraved on the panel recording the fact he was originally buried in Beaurains German Cemetery.

Stephen Dendrino 27 Squadron

On 27 September 1916 the Battle of the Somme was still in full swing, and at 0900 hours six Sopwith 1 1/2 Strutters, escorted by six Martinsyde scouts, set off on an Offensive Patrol. The object was to draw the enemy up to fight. The tactics worked only too well - unfortunately the formation ran into Oswald Boelcke, as described in *Knight of Germany* by Johannes Werner:

Stephen Dendrino.

> *I met another five Englishmen in the Bapaume area about midday on the 27th. I was on patrol with four of my gentlemen; when we reached the front, I saw a squadron which I first took for a German formation. But when we met to the southeast of Bapaume, I recognised them for enemy aircraft. As we were lower than they, I turned away to northward. The Englishmen then passed by us, crossed our lines, circled round a bit behind our captive balloons and then wanted to go home. Meanwhile, however, we had climbed to their height and cut them off. I gave the signal to attack, and the fun started. It was a mighty scrap. I got to grips with one, and basted*

him properly, but came up too close and had to pass out below him. Then I went into a turn, in the course of which I saw the Englishmen go down and fall like a sack somewhere near Ervillers.

I engaged another immediately - there were plenty of them. He tried to get away from me, but it did not avail him - I hung on close behind all the time. Yet I was surprised by this opponent's tenacity - I thought I really must have settled him some time before, but he kept on flying round and round in the same sort of circles. At long last I could stand it no longer - I said to myself that the man must be dead and the controls are jammed so as to keep the machine in a normal position. So I flew quite close up to him - and then saw the man sprawling over in the cockpit, dead. I left the machine to its fate, having noted its number - 7495. When we got home, it came out that Sergeant Reimann had also shot down a machine that bore the number 7495. To avoid doing either of us an injustice the staff officer acted on my suggestion that the victory should not be credited to anyone.

After leaving No. 7495 I took on another. He got a good dose from me, but after a series of fighting turns managed to escape behind his own lines. When I had to pass out under him, I saw how my bullets had cut his fuselage about. He will remember that day for a long time! And so shall I, for I worked like a nigger and sweated like a reserve officer.

Reimann was the first *jasta* pilot to claim a victory and his career is described in *Airfields and Airmen, Cambrai,* page 37.

The first machine shot down, a Martinsyde of 27 Squadron, was flown by Henry Arthur Taylor, who was killed. He was buried initially in Ervillers German Cemetery but today lies in Mory Abbey Military Cemetery, south of Arras. Taylor had been appointed a flight commander only two days before he was killed, and had been awarded an MC for a bombing raid.

The second machine shot down was Stephen Dendrino. He was born on 16 March 1889 and had a Greek father, with whom he had little contact in later life. Educated at Southgate School and the Thames Nautical Training College, he joined the merchant navy, becoming a third officer with the

Martinsyde 7498 of 27 Squadron missing on 24 September 1916. The pilot, Second Lieutenant E N Wingfield was taken prisoner. It was later flown by the Germans.

Peninsular and Oriental Service. In October 1914 he was involved in transport work in German East Africa and directing troops under fire on the SS *Karuala.*

Applying to the RFC in February 1916, he was appointed a flying officer on 3 August 1916. After his fateful meeting with Boelcke, his machine gently circled until it eventually made a reasonably soft landing on the German side.

An interesting observation concerning security is that, despite exhortations not to carry items useful to the enemy, many aircrew still did. In January 1918 the Germans forwarded Dendrino's personal effects which consisted of driving licence, driver's card, cheque book, letters, visiting cards and a receipt.

Return north on the D5 and continue ahead over a roundabout until you turn right on the N17 into Arras. Pass over the railway bridge to the traffic lights, then turn left on the dual carriageway. The cemetery will appear on the left.

Faubourg d'Amiens Cemetery

The British part of this cemetery (10/1) was begun in March 1916 behind the French military cemetery and was in continuous use until the Armistice. It was enlarged post-war by the inclusion of battlefield casualties and by graves from two other smaller cemeteries. The French graves were later removed and the area they occupied was employed to build the Arras Memorial and the Air Forces Memorial to the Missing.

The Arras Memorial commemorates the 35,000 men from the UK, South Africa and New Zealand who were killed between the spring of 1916 and 7 August 1918. The Canadian unknowns are commemorated at Vimy, and the Australians at Villers-Bretonneux. There are about 2,600 First World War burials here, though there are only five aviators, of which one is a very interesting German one.

The grave we have come to pay our respects to is in the small German plot on the far side of the cemetery from the Air Services Memorial.

Leutnant Paul Vogel *Jasta* 23b

Vogel was born on 8 October 1894 in Roda. After service in Infantry Regiment No. 9 he joined the air service.

Posted to *Jasta* 23b, a Bavarian unit on 4 May 1918, he suffered a number of mishaps, from which he escaped with his life. On 12 July he was wounded and then on 25 July, he was shot down in flames, the most dreaded of all fates feared by airmen during the Great War. Fortunately, the Germans had started introducing the Heinecke parachute in limited numbers in early spring 1918 and one of these saved Vogel's life. A significant number of lives were spared using this basic device, including Ernst Udet who finished the war as Germany's highest scoring living ace.

Five days later Vogel was shot down in flames again, and once more his parachute saved him. Awarded the Iron Cross First Class, Vogel was living on borrowed time. On 15 September he was in combat with No. 1 Squadron RAF and was shot down into the Allied lines, later dying of his wounds. His aeroplane was a Pfalz DXII, the only one of its type to fall into British hands before the war ended, and thus of intense interest to intelligence.

Rudolf Stark, commander of the Bavarian *Jasta* 35b, in his book *Wings of War* described his view of the Pfalz DXII:

1.9.18.

We are to have more new machines. Everyone is pleased, especially the pilots who have not yet got their Fokkers. But their joy is soon damped down, for the machines allotted to them are not Fokkers, but Pfalz D.12s.

What is a Pfalz D.12? No one has ever heard of such a machine, no one knows anything about it.

We decline to take these machines. The result is a series of long telephone conversations; we are told that they are very good, better than Fokkers in some respects (eyewash!), and we must take them.

Jagdgruppe 8B, a Bavarian formation, consisting of *Jastas* 23, 34 and 35. At the front is *Hauptmann* Eduard von Schleich, commanding the unit, and sixth from the left is Paul Vogel.

There are no more Fokkers to be had, and in any case these new Pfalzs are better than the old Albatroses, and when new Fokkers come along, we can take them in exchange.

All right; then we'll have the Pfalzs.

We go along to the park and take over the machines. The sight of them does not inspire much confidence; the fuselage and controls are the usual kinds, the wings are somewhat compacter, with a multitude of bracing wires. The whole contrivance looks just like a harp. We are spoilt for such machines, because we are too much accustomed to the unbraced Fokker wings.

Each of us climbed into the new machines with a prejudice against them and immediately tried to find as many faults as possible. The Staffel's opinion was the same as ours. The works sergeant grumbled because of the trouble the bracing was going to make for him while the mechanics cursed because of the extra work to assemble and dismantle them and declared them awkward to handle. No one wanted to fly those Pfalzs except under compulsion, and those who had to made as much fuss as they could about practising on them.

Later their pilots got on very well with them. They flew quite decently and could always keep pace with the Fokkers; in fact they dived even faster. But they were heavy for turns and fighting purposes, in which respect they were not to be compared with the Fokkers. The Fokker was a bloodstock animal that answered to the slightest movement of hand and could almost guess the rider's will in advance. The Pfalz was a clumsy cart-horse that went heavy in the reins and obeyed nothing but the most brutal force.

Those who flew the Pfalzs did so because there were no other machines for them. But they always gazed enviously at the Fokkers and prayed for the quick chance of an exchange.

On 15 September 1918 No. 1 Squadron RAF, mounted an Offensive Patrol, which included the commanding officer, Major W E Young, who had flown with Mannock in 74 Squadron. Seventeen SE5as attacked a mixed formation of Fokkers and other enemy aircraft. Lieutenant D E Cameron reported:

5.05 pm 12000' D E Cameron
  Single seater (type unknown)
At 5.05 pm our patrol attacked a number

Bristol Fighter E2580 'C' of A Flight, 62 Squadron.

of Fokker and other EA scouts at 12000'. I observed one diving on the tail of an SE and I turned and followed EA down. The EA attempted to shake me off by half rolls and turns but I got in half a dozen good bursts until within 100 feet of the ground.

I then observed the EA strike the ground and turn on its back near Recourt. I fired 120 rounds.

William Newby from the 1 Squadron patrol had to land within 500 yards of the crashed enemy machine due to engine trouble. The German aeroplane had also been shot at by a Bristol Fighter of 62 Squadron, flown by Captain W E Staton and his observer Lieutenant L E Mitchell. The Bristol landed near the crash and Staton and Newby walked across to see it. The following day Young wrote a letter to Headquarters 9 Brigade:

Although they arrived within 10 minutes of the EA crashing they found that the infantry had removed all the instruments, black crosses, magnetos and a large portion of the fabric and 3-ply. Lt. Newby was able to secure the parachute.

No units were identified except the 93rd Battery R.F.A. 56th Division, who looked after Lt. Newby till a tender from here reached him. The infantry appeared to be mostly Canadian - officers and men.

The E.A. was of an unknown type and the parts cut away by the infantry would probably be of the utmost value in determining details of the design.

Can steps be taken, please to try and recover some of these parts?

If the machine had been left untouched, it could have been salved practically intact.

Apart from the items listed by Young, the troops had also taken the undercarriage and both guns. Unfortunately, looting of crashed enemy machines was a perennial problem on the British side, from which the Germans did not seem to suffer. Much valuable intelligence was lost this way. You only need to see pictures of the remains of Manfred von Richthofen's triplane, which landed almost intact, to see the size of the problem.

Vogel's Pfalz DXII photographed at No. 2 Aeroplane Supply Depot. This clearly shows the damage caused by souvenir hunters.

The official technical intelligence report was published only nine days later, and included several photographs illustrating how much damage had occurred in only ten minutes. The report also commented on the accuracy of the 1 Squadron gunnery:

> *It is interesting to note that our pilots made some excellent shooting during the combat, there being a group of shots about 12" in diameter through the 3-ply at the back of the pilot's seat, and a similar group on the starboard side of the fuselage about 18" behind the pilot's seat. There were no signs of bullet holes in the fabric of the planes.*

Staton admitted his guns had jammed and at that time the unidentified machine was still under control, so he therefore made no claim for it. However, he later changed his story and it was credited to both squadrons.

The victors: D E Cameron

Douglas Ewan Cameron was born on 18 January 1893 and came from Southampton. Attending Glasgow University from 1910 until August 1914, he graduated with an MA. In January 1918 he was posted to No. 1 School of Military Aeronautics and after tuition at 28 Training Squadron he joined 1 Squadron on 15 June 1918. After his Vogel combat, he shared in an out of control, possibly crashed enemy machine on 28 October. On 6 January 1919 he was posted out of 1 Squadron and demobilised five days later. In June 1919 he was Mentioned in Despatches.

W E Staton

William Ernest Staton, or 'Bull' as he was known, was born on 27 August 1898. He joined 62 Squadron, flying the Bristol Fighter, where he teamed up with his observer, Lieutenant J R Gordon. He claimed his first victory, a Fokker Triplane, out of control, on 13 March 1918. In August and September he flew with a number of gunners, until acquiring a regular one in Lieutenant L E Mitchell. By the end of the war he was 62 Squadron's most successful pilot with 26 victories, having been awarded an MC, DFC and bar.

Remaining in the RAF, he was a wing commander in charge of 10 Squadron when the Second World War started. The award of a DSO was promulgated in

183

W E Staton (left) and his observer J R Gordon on 1 May 1918 in front of Bristol Fighter C4619.

1940. As Senior Air Staff Officer in Singapore, he was taken prisoner by the Japanese in 1942 and suffered great privation in their hands. He was Mentioned in Despatches for his services while a prisoner. After the war various command appointments followed, and he retired in 1952, as an air vice-marshal, having been awarded a CB. A keen shot, he was Captain of the British Shooting Teams in the 1948 and 1952 Olympics. He died in Emsworth, Hampshire on 22 July 1983.

L E Mitchell

Leslie Edwin Mitchell was not to enjoy his moment of glory for long, as two weeks later while he was flying with Lieutenant R H O'Reilly on a Line Patrol, their machine was seen to break up, possibly hit by a shell and they were killed. Both are buried at Rumaucourt Communal Cemetery, southeast of Arras.

Postscript

Vogel's machine was allocated the number G/HQ/6 and it was delivered from 1 Squadron to No.2 Salvage Dump a week later. Newby retrieved the parachute from the Pfalz and, as some parachutes were used more than once, it may very well have been the one that had saved Vogel on the two previous occasions. The rudder from his machine is in 1 Squadron's museum alongside that taken from the Fokker Triplane captured on 9 June 1918 (see page 117). The cover of the *Windsock Datafile* featuring the Pfalz DXII has a splendid Brian Knight painting of the Vogel combat. See Further Reading.

The author (left) and the noted aviation writer Norman Franks at RAF Wittering in 2000 with the rudder from Paul Vogel's Pfalz.

PFALZ D12.
15th Sept 1918.

The Air Forces Memorial to the Missing

I tend to be rather ambivalent about this memorial. Firstly, at least there is a separate memorial for the RFC, RNAS and RAF missing, which is only right and just. However, it does not do justice to the sacrifice or memory of these men. It is hardly more imposing than a number of divisional memorials scattered along the Western Front. Secondly, why is it in the middle of Arras? I understand that being in the centre of the British front was a consideration but why not place it in a far more historic and relevant aviation-related place, such as the aerodrome at St Omer? Just about every member of the RFC passed through No. 1 Aircraft Depot, many of them a number of times. It was the spiritual home of the RFC and the funnel through which the material and men poured through. Thousands of men were employed here.

At the time of writing (January 2004), under the auspices of *Cross and Cockade*, and the leadership of its president, Air Commodore Peter Dye, funds are being collected to erect a fitting memorial on this site due for opening in 2004, which will be the 90th anniversary of the RFC landing in France.

The opening of the Air Services Memorial at Arras was scheduled for Sunday, 15 May 1932. Unfortunately, the President of the French Republic died and the ceremony was delayed until Sunday 31 July. As the RAF did not have a memorial in France, the War Office generously stepped aside and regarded the unveiling of the Arras memorial as an RAF occasion. Over 5,000 people attended, mostly veterans and their families. The hot sun shone fitfully through great white clouds. The Prefect of the Somme was welcomed by Sir Fabian Ware, representing the Imperial War Graves Commission. The Air Forces memorial was unveiled by Marshal of the Royal Air Force Lord Trenchard, who laid a wreath in his capacity as unveiling officer, though the wreath on behalf of the RAF was laid by Air Vice-Marshal H C T Dowding. Music was provided by the thirty-six musicians of the RAF Central Band. Three pipers of the Seaforth Highlanders marched across the apse in slow time playing *The Flowers of the Forest*. Five Fairey IIIFs of 24 Squadron, which had flown the RAF senior officers from the UK, flew a formation flypast. The following day Trenchard was the RAF representative at the unveiling of the Thiepval Memorial by the Prince of Wales, the last official British memorial to be dedicated on the Western Front.

Air Mechanic Second Class H H Bright

On the Air Services Memorial there are about 1,000 names of RFC, RNAS and RAF personnel with no known grave. On the side facing you as you approach the memorial are recorded members of the RFC, with Lanoe Hawker VC as the top name and then descending in rank order. The right face of the monument records the balance of the RFC casualties. The back face has the names of the RAF casualties with the top name being Major R R Barker and the next Major Mick Mannock VC (see page 113 and *Ypres* page 106). The left face has the balance of the RAF missing, plus those of Canada, Australia, New Zealand, South Africa and India.

On the right hand side of the monument almost at the bottom is the name of Air Mechanic Second Class H H Bright who was the only air mechanic killed as a pilot in the British flying service and his story is a sad one.

SE5 A8918 'W' of 60 Squadron, showing the squadron marking of a white disc. Second Lieutenant H T Hammond was taken prisoner of war on 14 September 1917.

Horatio Harle Bright was born on 26 August 1898, at Ecclesall Bierlow, Sheffield. He attended Sherborne Preparatory School and Marlborough and was still at school in October 1914. Volunteering for the RFC, he was instructed to join at Brooklands on 1 July 1915. He was posted to Netheravon on 11 August 1915 but the War Office did not realise he was only sixteen years of age! Correspondence passed between the Deputy Director of Military Aeronautics, Bright's father and the Royal Aero Club. His father wrote to the military, stating he would not attribute any blame upon the government if his son was injured, as long as he could continue flying. The Royal Aeronautical Club was prepared to issue Bright's 'ticket' if the War office accepted him.

In the event, the powers-that-be declined, and Bright's Royal Aero Club certificate, No. 1648, was issued on his 17th birthday, 26 August 1915. He graduated from CFS on 19 October and arrived in France on 29 October with a posting to 6 Squadron RFC. After six months with them he joined 1 Squadron but was only there for two weeks, before transferring to 29 Squadron. Hospitalised in July and September, he left this unit on 6 September 1916 for a medical board.

After a bout of influenza, he joined the Aeronautical Inspection Department at Filton, near Bristol, as a test pilot, on Boxing Day 1916.

Unfortunately, for reasons unknown, Bright's behaviour became erratic. There were complaints of extremely dangerous flying, such that he was, after several warnings, forbidden to fly by the officer commanding Filton. He was also forbidden to use the officer's mess on account of passing worthless cheques and was taking women into Filton and giving them unofficial flights. In addition, he was absent on a number of occasions. On 29 May 1917 he was arrested and three days later tried by General Court-

Martial. There were two charge sheets, involving a total of eight charges. Four of these involved having in his possession photographs of various parts of Filton and Bristol, then showing them to unauthorised individuals in such a way that it was calculated *to be useful to the enemy*. Of the eight charges, he was convicted of six of them. He was sentenced to be cashiered and imprisoned for twelve months without hard labour.

On the recommendation of General Officer Commanding, Southern Command, the imprisonment was remitted due to Bright's young age and war service and the fact that there was no traitorous intent. As for the photography charges, he was deemed to have behaved with *extraordinary folly.*

On 23 August the Director of Recruiting, 16th Recruiting Area, at Bedford, attempted to contact Bright but he had already enlisted in the RFC and on 6 September 1917 proceeded to France.

Joining 60 Squadron at Ste-Marie-Cappel he carried out his first practice flight on 22 September. Later that day

Keith 'Grid' Caldwell (left) who was leading the patrol in which Bright was lost. While serving in 8, 60 and 74 Squadrons he claimed twenty-five victories and earned an MC, DFC and bar. He reached the rank of air commodore in the Royal New Zealand Air Force.

he flew an Offensive Patrol, from which he had to return temporarily, due to Vickers machine-gun trouble. In the evening he delivered a new machine from No. 1 Aircraft Depot, St Omer to the squadron. At 0900 hours the next day, he left on a five-man patrol, led by the great New Zealand ace Captain Grid Caldwell, from which he failed to return. Nobody saw what happened to him and there does not seem to be a relevant claim from the German side. A sad end to a very sad story.

Return to the centre of Arras. This concludes the third and final tour of Airfields and Airmen: Arras.

Conclusion

For those readers whose interest in First War aviation may have been aroused by this present book I can recommend joining *Cross and Cockade International - The First World War Aviation Historical Society*. Since publication of *Airfields and Airmen: Cambrai* the membership secretary's address has changed to:

Membership Secretary
Cross and Cockade International
11 Francis Drive
Westward Ho!
EX39 1XE
e-mail: cci@blueyonder.co.uk

Their website is http://www.crossandcockade.com

I can also recommend *Over the Front*, the journal of The League of World War 1 Aviation Historians. Their membership secretary's address has also changed and is:

Membership Secretary
The League of World War 1 Aviation Historians
16820 25th Ave. N.
Plymouth
MN 55447-2228
e-mail: dpolglaze@comcast.net
Their website is http://www.overthefront.com

In addition, I am always interested in contacting First World War aviators or their relatives, whether they figure in the *Airfields and Airmen* series of books or not. My e-mail address is:
oconnor@stonehousecottage.freeserve.co.uk

Further Reading

A Selected Bibliography
Courage Remembered, Kingsley Ward and E Gibson, HMSO 1989.
The Sky Their Battlefield, Trevor Henshaw, Grub Street 1995.
Airmen Died in the Great War, Chris Hobson, Hayward and Son 1995.
Under the Guns of the German Aces, N Franks and H Giblin, Grub Street 1997.
Pfalz DXII, Windsock Datafile No. 41, P M Grosz, Albatros Productions Ltd 1993
Naval Eight, edited by E G Johnstone, Arms and Armour Press 1972.
Albert Ball VC, Chaz Bowyer, William Kimber and Co 1977.
For Valour The Air VC's, Chaz Bowyer.,William Kimber and Co 1978.
High in the Empty Blue, The History of 56 Squadron RFC/RAF 1916-1919, Alex Revell, Flying Machines Press 1995.
Years of Combat, Sholto Douglas, Collins 1963.
Flying Corps Headquarters 1914-18, Maurice Baring, William Heinemann 1930.
The Red Air Fighter, M von Richthofen, The Aeroplane and General Publishing Co 1918.
The Red Knight of Germany, Floyd Gibbons, Cassell 1930.
The Red Baron Combat Wing, Peter Kilduff, Arms and Armour 1997.
Hawker VC , Tyrrel M Hawker, Mitre Press 1965.
Ace of the Iron Cross, Ernst Udet, Newnes 1937.
War in an Open Cockpit, G W Callender Jr and Sr, WW1 Aero Publishers 1978.
The Red Baron's Last Flight, N Franks and A Bennett, Grub Street 1997.
Flying Fury, J T B McCudden, John Hamilton 1930.
Germany's Last Knight of the Air, Editor P Kilduff, William Kimber 1979
King of Air Fighters, J I T Jones, Ivor Nicholson and Watson 1934.
Wings over the Somme, G H Lewis, William Kimber 1976.
No Parachute, A S G Lee, Jarrolds Publishers 1968.
I Chose the Sky, L H Rochford, William Kimber 1977.
Fighter Pilot, McScotch, Newnes, No date.
Skill and Devotion, P E Butcher, radio Modeller Book Division 1971.
Knight of Germany, J Werner, Hamilton 1933.
Casualties of the German Air Service, Franks, Bailey and Duiven, Grub Street 1999.
Wings of War, Rudolf Stark, John Hamilton Ltd 1933.
The Courage of the Early Morning, W A Bishop, William Heinemann 1966.
Winged Warfare, W A Bishop, Hodder and Staughton 1918.
Flying and Soldiering, R R Money, Ivor Nicholson 1936.
Pictorial History of the German Army Air Service, Alex Imrie, Ian Allan 1971.
The Royal Flying Corps in France, Ralph Barker (two volumes), Constable 1994 and 1995.
The Jasta Pilots, Franks/Bailey/Duiven, Grub Street 1996.
Above the Trenches, Shores/Franks/Guest, Grub Street 1990.
Above the Lines, Franks/Bailey/Guest, Grub Street 1993.
Bloody April, Alan Morris, Jarrolds 1967.
The Fokker Triplane, Alex Imrie, Arms and Armour 1992.
The Mad Major, Major Christopher Draper DSC, Air Review Ltd 1962.
Number One in War and Peace, Norman Franks and Mike O'Connor, Grub Street 2000.
The Aeroplanes of the Royal Flying Corps (Military Wing), J M Bruce, Putnams 1982.
Zeppelin! Ray L Rimell, Conway Maritime Press 1984.

INDEX